CULTURE SHOCK!

china

Kevin Sinclair
with Iris Wong Po-yee

TIMES BOOKS INTERNATIONAL
Singapore • Kuala Lumpur

Illustrations by TRIGG
Photographs by Kevin Sinclair
Cover photographs by Luca I. Tettoni

© 1990 Kevin Sinclair

This book is published by
Times Books International,
an imprint of Times Editions Pte Ltd
Times Centre, 1 New Industrial Road
Singapore 1953
2nd Floor, Wisma Hong Leong Yamaha
50 Jalan Penchala, 46050 Petaling Jaya
Selangor, Malaysia

Printed by Jin Jin Printing Industry Pte Ltd

ISBN 981 204 080 3

To Kit, my wife and companion on journeys along the China Coast.

And to Iris Wong Po-yee, who has been with me to ports, paddyfields, coal mines, steel works, kindergartens, factories, vegetable farms, plantations and shipyards in every province between Guangdong and the Mongol border.

And to Lui Kamwing in Hongkong, He Zhiquan in Guangzhou, Shen Dexiang in Shanghai, He Hualin in Beijing and thousands of other friends in cities, villages and farms throughout China with whom I have shared long conversations, pleasant meals and frequent toasts of *mao-tai*.

PREFACE

When I first came to the China coast more than a half lifetime ago, it was a journey spurred by curiosity. As a boy in far-distant New Zealand, I had gone to school with Chinese. I hadn't taken much notice of them; they were just other kids in the class who happened to be a bit different from the white Anglo-Saxons, the Greeks, the native Maoris, the Indians and the Pacific Islanders. When I was 14 I withdrew a book from the mobile library which made weekly visits to the farm area where my family lived. The volume was called *Red Star Over China* and it was the epic account of how Mao Zedong and the starving, desperate Red Army had walked across China towards their vision of the future. By that stage, the mid-1950s, China was going through its turbulent course of struggling towards the utopia of perfect communism, towards a society in which everyone would be equal. It was a nice idea. Pity it never worked.

But that book had planted a germ which was to flourish a decade later when I arrived in Hongkong as a newspaperman. I came down the gangplank of the corrosive old liner berthed at Kowloon docks, looked around, smelled the fried bean curd, saw the stunning height of the cloud-wreathed pinnacle of The Peak—and promptly fell in love. My first job was on *The Star*. It was a bouncy tabloid, outrageous not in bare breasts but in taking on powerful enemies. The Cultural Revolution had erupted in China and the revolutionary fury had washed over into the streets of Hongkong. They were filled with tear gas, running with blood. The war was raging in Vietnam and down in Suzie Wong's neon world of Wanchai, the bars were heaving as young American soldiers took brief respite from the jungles of Vietnam. It was an exciting time to be a reporter.

But it was events over the border in China that held me in great fascination. From camouflaged spy posts atop mountain crests, I watched as Red Guards paraded down the dykes in the rice paddies and as unfortunates caught trying to escape to Hongkong were dragged away to a knoll known as Execution Hill to be dispatched by murder squads. What made this country tick? How could a people so civilised, so urbane, so talented fall victim to such mass insanity? Why did Chinese people act like this? What made these mysterious Chinese in China so different to the Chinese friends I had swiftly made in Hongkong and other Chinese I had known years earlier in New Zealand, Australia and Singapore?

It was to be many years before I first got permission to enter China and could start trying to answer such baffling queries for myself. Since then, I have made more than 80 visits to many provinces. Perhaps I am beginning to edge a little closer to the enigma of why going to China is such a culture shock for so many.

CONTENTS

FOREWORD

To learn what is good, a thousand days are not sufficient
To learn what is evil, an hour is too long.

The Chinese are different. Ask any of the 1,127,000,000 people who live in the world's most populous country and they will cheerfully agree. The vast sweep of Chinese history, the country's inward-looking culture, the ethnocentrism of the Han Chinese who make up 93 per cent of the population, have combined to produce a civilisation that regards itself as being not only culturally unique, but uniquely superior.

The poorest coolie humping sacks of rice on the Ningbo waterfront is convinced in his own mind of his inherent pre-eminence over any millionaire, professor or politician of any other nation. Why not? He's Chinese, isn't he? As such, he feels the direct cultural beneficiary of philosophers like Confucius and Lao Tzu, rulers such as Qin Shihuang—the great unifier who first brutally and efficiently forged the nation into one empire 2,200 years ago— and writers and poets like Li Bai and Do Fu.

The well-dressed westerner in the expensive clothes and holding the camera that costs more than the average Chinese earns in a year may be a neurosurgeon from a famous hospital. But he's only a foreigner, for all that.

The Middle Kingdom

China is not just a country. In the 5,000 years since the first recognisably Chinese agricultural-based civilisation formed in the great bend of the Yellow River, it has developed into a distinctive civilisation. Through invasions, revolutions, disasters, the rise and collapse of dynasties, plagues, floods and famines, that civilisation has been kept more or less intact. A visitor from the Tang Dynasty whisked through time to the present could recognise his own rich legacy on the streets of any modern Chinese city. It is the world's oldest lifestyle.

China; the very name illustrates the Chinese outlook, the conviction of supremacy. The name comes from the two characters written in the *pinyin* modern version of Anglicised Chinese as Zhong Guo. This means, simply, the Central Nation, the Middle Kingdom of legend. To the Chinese, modern as well as ancient, their realm is the centre of the universe. Outside the pale of imperial domain dwelt the ignorant, slothful, pitied barbarians. These savages might intermittently swarm down over the Great Wall to subjugate huge swathes of China, to lay waste the land, to plunder its treasures, even to ascend for centuries to the Dragon Throne. But they were still outsiders, still to be looked down on because they were not blessed by being Chinese.

The Onlookers

It is to help those going to China to see the ancient land and to meet its engaging and often baffling people, that this book is aimed. Understanding China and the Chinese is never easy. The language barrier, for a start, stands awesomely in the way of most visitors from abroad. But, language aside, there are still significant differences in outlook, manner, work ethics, eating, entertainment, dress, ways of relaxing and even in such simple areas as saying hello that make Chinese different from much of the rest of the world.

Hopefully, this book will help unlock some of the loops in this complex Chinese puzzle.

Chapter One

CHINA TODAY

Once the dragon gate is crossed,
One's status rises ten times.

China is changing today faster than at any time in her long history.
The pace is blinding. New economic policies are being implemented
that the rulers in Beijing predict confidently will make the country
one of the world's leading economic powers in the 21st century.
The opportunities are great. So are the problems. The potential is
enormous. So are the economic hurdles that have to be overcome.
Even more daunting are the political chasms; hesitant moves towards

liberalism were crushed in June 1989, along with the bodies of students in Tiananmen Square.

Despite political upheavals, change is inevitably taking place in the world's oldest civilisation. A new generation of eager young technocrats is taking charge in China. It is like a marathon relay race; the old runners who have been carrying the baton since the time of the Long March in the 1930s are now handing it on to new leaders born since the establishment of Communist China in 1949. It is a transition spanning more than a generation; the flame is being passed from the revolutionaries who marched with Mao to men and women who learned to use computers while they studied for their MBAs in Stanford or Edinburgh. It's a whole new world.

Perhaps. But in huge swathes of China, the past lives on. No matter what policies are laid down in distant Beijing, despite the emergence of Guangzhou as one of the most vital manufacturing cities on earth and Shanghai throwing off the sloth of decades to become a powerhouse to generate industry for half a continent, down in the countryside, Chinese life remains basically uninterrupted.

A Great Leap—Backwards

The Great Leap Forward and the Great Proletarian Cultural Revolution—two of the greatest man-made disasters in history— took millions of peasant lives. Like tidal waves, earthquakes and droughts, these calamities swept over the Chinese peasants who struggled once again to the surface to patiently rebuild their lives.

Since 1911, the nation has undergone enormous, fundamental changes. In that year, after decades of unrest, the Chinese people arose and overthrew the Manchus of the Qing Dynasty who had sat on the Dragon Throne since 1644. Instead of a brave new world of egalitarian rule leading towards prosperity and freedom from foreign oppression, the long-awaited revolution instead ushered in the convulsions of the warlord era. The country was weakened, split, fractured as squabbling local dictators imposed corrupt and selfish

11

rule on many parts of the country.

Dr Sun Yat-sen, inspiration for modern China, died before he could see his dream of a unified nation come true. The inheritor of his vision, Generalissimo Chiang Kai-shek, grasped briefly at the chance to weld the country into one modern nation. In 1928, he led the Great Northern Expedition to unseat the warlords from Beijing. He conquered all that stood before him and, briefly, China had hope.

Then the Kuomintang (National Party) of Chiang Kai-shek split with another group of ardent reformists, the communists (or *gongchantang*) and the civil war started that was to drag on for two decades. Simultaneously, a much more brutal threat afflicted China. In 1932, the Japanese had driven into the rich industrial plains of Manchuria, seizing the three strategic provinces. Five years later, they struck into the heart of China. For eight more years, the country was torn apart by vicious foreign invasion and brutal occupation and by civil war. When Japan surrendered in 1945, the Kuomintang had largely discredited its mandate from the people; corruption, nepotism, inflation and greed had eaten away at its foundations.

In the final stages of the civil war, the communist armies hammered down the length of China from their northern strongholds, joining with local militias and underground bands in the rural areas and with workers and students who welcomed them in the cities. By 1 October 1949, Chairman Mao Zedong and his victorious marshals could stand at the Gate of Heavenly Peace in Beijing and proclaim to the world the birth of the People's Republic of China.

Once again, early hopes were soon to lose much of their lustre. The communists accomplished much good. The land was redistributed basically on the lines of the slogan that had helped carry the Red Army to victory: 'The land to the sower.' But then this promise was largely negated; the landlords had been purged (often executed) and dispossessed. Instead, there was collectivisation. At first, the communes worked. Over the years they became inefficient.

Chairman Mao Zedong is remembered as a great leader. His successors admit his victories were tempered by 'many mistakes', but his statues still dominate many towns, his face still looks enigmatically out over Tiananmen Square.

The legendary productivity of the Chinese peasant drooped. Politically and economically, the government blundered time and time again. A 'hundred flowers' of intellectual freedom were urged to bloom; when the flowers put their heads up in the thaw, they were swiftly plucked. A 'great leap forward' was proclaimed with peasants urged to forge foundries, feed furnaces in their rural plots. It was

13

disastrous. Crops suffered and at least three million people starved to death in the unwise man-made famine.

Great Helmsman Loses Grip

And then, growing feeble and desperate to preserve the purity of his revolution, in 1966, Mao, the Great Helmsman, steered his people into the most extraordinary peril. He called on the youth of China to arise, to wipe out the Four Olds of Old Ideas, Old Culture, Old Customs and Old Habits, and to cleanse the nation in renewed revolutionary fire. Even 20 years after the peak of its fury, nobody could estimate how many people died in the relentless frenzy of the Great Proletarian Cultural Revolution. Certainly, it plunged China's progress back a thousand steps. It deprived a generation of schooling. It left its marks on millions of hearts. Scarcely a family in China was untouched somehow, sometime, in that black decade.

When it ended with the death of Mao and the arrest of his wife and other ultra-leftist leaders, the Cultural Revolution left China a shaken, poor nation. The country was like a sick patient recovering from a long and debilitating illness.

A new wave of leaders took power in the Forbidden City. Like Mao, they were old revolutionaries who had tramped on the Long March, who had fought Japanese and Kuomintang, who had suffered the deprivations in the cave city of Yanan which was their wartime base. They had won their laurels, wore them proudly. But their vision of the new China was not one of eternal revolution. Rather, they shared the dream of building a modern, industrialised society which could take its place in the world community.

The first outlines of how this could be achieved were disclosed by Deng Xiaoping in 1978. At the crucial foundation of these economic plans was the sturdy basis of Chinese riches for the preceding 5000 years; the farmers were to be set free from their cooperative chains to work for themselves. This simple policy had immediate and obvious results. Farmers worked best in family groups, the traditional basis of Chinese civilisation. Now that they could plant what they wished, sell for the best price on open markets, they went to work with a will. Within five years, agricultural production had doubled in value. The peasants prospered mightily. Water buffaloes plodding in sodden paddy fields began to give way to more efficient small tractors. Electricity came to the countryside. Farmers had television sets, rice cookers, watches, radios, bicycles. 'To be rich is glorious,' Deng Xiaoping preached. Few political slogans have been seized so eagerly, followed so enthusiastically.

In the cities, the obvious wealth of the peasants was envied. It was difficult to translate extra payments for hard work, initiative and productivity from farm to factory. Gradually, systems for profit sharing, for piece-work pay and hefty bonuses for results raised the pay for industrial workers. In turn, this led to more problems. In the past, since 1949, it had been an honour to serve in the armed forces and the government. Now, young people were not so eager to don uniform or to work in administrative jobs. During the time when all China was poor, it had been beneficial to be a bureaucrat. At least you had face, prestige, standing and the powers of office. But who wanted to sit down in an office earning RMB70 a month when a factory worker was earning three times as much, a free enterprise hawker on the streets could earn five times as much and a humble farmer planting pumpkins on the outskirts of a suburban city could earn the fantastic wage, for China, of RMB8000 a year? Where now was the attraction of being a soldier or a junior public servant following the communists' decree of Serve The People?

Attempting to bring some sort of balance to the national pay scales has been one of the major headaches caused by the new prosperity. It is a problem as yet unsolved. So is an efficient way to tackle inflation, a troubling worry to a government that had seen the preceding regime tumbled largely because skyrocketing inflation in 1948 had wiped out the urban middle class.

Alas, political developments lagged many *li* behind the swift pace of economic reform. In that other communist giant, the Soviet Union, energetic new leadership loosened the reins and allowed a long subjugated people to have their say. Russians had little on which to spend their worthless roubles, but they could complain about what they could not buy. In China, the shops were stocked with an astonishing range of consumer goods that would make Soviet citizens stare with envious disbelief. But the Chinese people remained firmly muzzled. Political dissent resulted in loss of jobs, persistence meant arrest, party discipline and a stretch in a dreaded political re-education camp.

Then, in April 1989, the former Communist Party secretary-general Hu Yaobang died. Students perceived Hu as a reformer who had tried to give China's brand of socialism a human face. They flocked to Tiananmen Square, spiritual heartland of the nation, to pay their respects. The gathering, as such meetings tend to do in China, acted as a magnet. Soon the vast square was thronged with shouting, wildly enthusiastic young people. From mourning Hu, it developed into a re-creation of the May 4th protests of 1929 when students demonstrated against the corruption, inefficiency and dictatorship of a former regime. A much vaunted ceremonial reception for Soviet leader Mikhail Gorbachev was thrown into political shadow.

Hiding in Forbidden City

In their homes alongside the Forbidden City, the party leaders fumed. They had lost enormous amounts of face. But to try to placate the students, leaders such as Zhao Ziyang and Li Peng went to the square to beg and persuade demonstrators to call off their protests and to meet to discuss grievances at a later date. All such moves failed. Attempts to break up the demonstrations with police action failed. Law enforcement men were beaten up. Then the military was called in.

The People's Liberation Army had been for four decades the most respected arm of government, seen as being above politics, as uncorruptible, as the army of the people, for the people. At first, as tens of thousands of Beijingers took to the streets, the army lived up to its proud reputation. Tanks ground to a halt in front of stand-fast demonstrators. Soldiers grinned at students calling for political changes to the communist system. Then roughnecks and hoodlums began attacking soldiers. More than 1000 automatic rifles were seized from troops who were under strict orders that they were under no circumstances to fire on the crowds.

Once again, appeals were made to the student demonstrators. Once again, troops attempting to reach the historic square were stopped in their tank tracks by huge crowds. In isolated incidents, unruly youths attacked unarmed soldiers sent to break up the demonstrations. Some soldiers were lynched, others kicked to death.

Eight long weeks after the first demonstrators flocked into the square, party patience had run out. The best efforts of the conciliators had failed. The tough old soldiers who had led the Red Army to victory two generations earlier came out of retirement and in party caucus voted for the steel fist to be withdrawn from the silken glove.

Then the tanks were ordered to roll again. This time, demonstrators who stood in the way were crushed. Into Tiananmen rumbled the People's Army. Out of the square fled the people. Overnight, China had changed yet again, making yet another of the dramatic diversions in her political course that have so often marked her long and turbulent history.

The immediate upshot of the short, torrid Summer of the Students was a hard and sweeping re-imposition of tough central party control. What the long-term implications will be is something that will not be evident for many years.

What's It All Mean?

So how do these tumultuous events affect visitors to China? Probably not a lot. The instant reaction of visitors at the time was to stay away in droves but even as the purge of intellectuals continued after the Tiananmen Incident, travellers were heading back to Beijing. In the south, production in the booming export-oriented factories hardly skipped a beat.

Western visitors to China should be careful how they raise such topics as the Chinese quest for democracy, the student uprising and the manner in which the Beijing spring was doused by the Chinese government. This is not for any fear that a communist secret policeman may be peering over your shoulder. He isn't. There are no bogeymen spying on your every word. (The fear of an omniscient Big Brother who keeps an efficient watchful eye on everyone in the land is not true. Chinese police and security forces are as inefficient, over-manned and incompetent as most branches of that stifling bureaucracy.)

There will be no repercussions against any tourist no matter what ill-advised and controversial questions he may ask or what anti-government expressions he may make. But the average Chinese is very wary of discussing such matters. With good reason. Even if he listens to a foreigner creating a diatribe against the leaders of the party and nation, he can place himself in peril of undergoing criticism and re-education. Just by being present when such criticism is voiced can place a Chinese in jeopardy.

So take care in what you say. Nobody is expecting you to parrot the self-praise of the Chinese government in 'putting down the counter-revolutionary uprising' which is how the massacre in Beijing is officially described. However, realise that any outright criticism of the government and the party will be intensely embarrassing to Chinese tour guides and others you might meet on your travels. You will put them in a situation where they will feel great unease and distress. Even if they secretly agree with you, as is likely, they will be unable to say so.

Ask questions, by all means, in your attempt to get an explanation

Inscrutable? What do you think? Cantonese girls giggle and squeal at the rare sight of a foreign devil carefully cleaning his antique car. When a string of 20 old vehicles head into China every spring as part of the Hongkong Chinese Car Club's annual rally, it is a true culture shock for peasants in country towns. They gather by the astonished thousands to watch as the gleaming procession splashes through rural lanes.

of the events that baffled and stunned the world. But don't expect a tour guide to come out with a denunciation of the Chinese government and a well-considered statement in support of the Bill of Rights and one-man, one-vote democracy.

Anyway, it's their country and if they want to run it as a one-party dictatorship, what's it got to do with you? How would you like it if someone from a completely different culture—say a socialist military regime—landed on your front door and began questioning the very fabric of your society? You might well ask yourself: 'Who

19

does this person think he is and what right has he got to be in my country as a guest demanding that I explain why I am not like him?' The Chinese you meet may well have a similar reaction to westerners who ask why China is not a liberal democratic country.

The Chinese Onion

China is like an onion. Observe it. Then peel off the outer skin. It looks the same. Peel off layer after layer. It still looks identical. But beneath each layer, as the observer penetrates deeper towards the inner core, there are subtle differences.

Most people will get only two or three layers deep. In doing so, they will see the patterns of the land and the people familiar to television viewers, the bamboo and the paddy fields, the immense bustling cities and the grandeur of the landscape, the pagodas poking through the mist and the Great Wall snaking over the eroded hills of Hebei.

Deep within the onion is the inner self of China. This is a lot more difficult to grasp.

It is easy, on a casual basis, to meet people in China. When you strive to speak basic Chinese, they will praise your efforts and your ability with the language. As your grasp of Chinese increases and—as a resident in the country, after a couple of years of study—you become more proficient, speaking with easy fluency about matters such as politics and philosophy, this praise for your linguistic ability becomes tinged with caution. This is particularly so among officials and intellectuals. Is the foreign devil getting too close to the kernel of how China works and how the Chinese people think?

The earlier enthusiasm with which hesitant language ability was praised now disappears. The foreigner's grasp of the language becomes a cause of worry, a source of fear and suspicion. Many foreigners who have gone through this process in China report that as their language ability increased it has become paradoxically more difficult for them to remain friends with Chinese to whom they thought they were growing close. Such are the complexities of a nation which has been ethnocentric and xenophobic for many centuries and for whose citizens friendship with foreigners has often meant persecution, prosecution or execution.

The outsider may be welcomed but is always mistrusted. The more relaxed and confident he becomes within Chinese society, all the more reason to distrust his intentions and to be wary of his capacity to slip towards the core of Chineseness like the worm into the apple. So say many who have spent the best part of their lives in China.

This complexity of knowledge is something which will not bother casual tourists or people who go to China to live and study for a few years. It is of concern more to the serious Sinologist whose life is strongly directed towards China and its development.

Chapter Two

THE PEOPLE

Sweat falling like rain, shoulders rubbing shoulders and toes touching heels.
— Poem from the Spring and Autumn period describing a multitude.

Old Hundred Names

The prosperity of China, now and through the ages, has rested always on the tough bent backs of the peasants. Ultimately, it was through their strong muscles, their patient skills, their endurance and strength, that the elegant civilisation of the cities was built. So

The eternal face of China, an old farmer plods home from the fields.

it remains today. Despite impressive advances over recent decades in industry, manufacturing and such elite fields as high-tech computers, it is the farmers on whom the basic economic might of the nation depends.

There are a lot of them. Although China now has to cope with some of the biggest cities in the world, more than 80 per cent of the population live in the countryside. Most live in villages where their ancestors toiled through the generations, bound in lifelong contracts to the soil. It is this vast majority of the people that is known as 'Old Hundred Names'. The term symbolises the mass of the Chinese peasantry working in idealised circumstances in a Confucian countryside of willow trees and dragon-backed bridges where everyone knows his place and happily keeps to it. Such a picture may be appealing; it is also largely imaginary.

Most peasants have had to stay down on the farm simply because there has been no alternative. This is changing as education becomes compulsory and universal; the degree of upward mobility may be slight but it is certainly more extensive than at any other time in China's long history.

Old Hundred Names? There are more like 5662 written Han Chinese surnames rather than 100. Many sound the same although they are written with different characters.

What's In A Name?

张　　王　　李　　赵　　刘

The five most common surnames, according to Chinese scholars, are Chang, Wang, Li, Chao and Liu. There are many millions of each. To be precise, social anthropologists tote up about 100 million Changs (or Chan in Cantonese) in modern China, about one in 12 of the population. They trace the character back to prehistoric times; it was common in the Jin territory four centuries before the Christian era. The character means 'to draw a bow'. So Mr Chang, in English, would be Mr Archer or Mr Bowman.

Similarly, many millions of one branch of the Wang clan can point to their character and claim to be descendants of emperors. Part of the character bears the symbol of imperial ruler. Rather like the Mr Kings of the western world. Lin, another common surname, has the character of three trees grouped together; if his ancestors had been English (perish the thought!) he would be Mr Forest or Wood.

Visitors can always ask Chinese to explain their names. Point to the topmost character on a business card (the family name) and ask what it means. They will be delighted to explain and consider you polite for having asked. Then they will ask the derivation of your family name. That's okay if you are called Ford or Smith or Butcher and if you can explain how the name developed. You might have a slight problem if you should have a surname like Kaszchenowski.

Who's Mr Li?

I was sitting in the Dragon Boat Bar of the Hongkong Hilton Hotel one day when a message boy marched between the tables with a small blackboard atop a mahogany pole. As he rang his bell to gain attention, people looked at the board to see who was wanted on the telephone. 'Mr Wong,' read the notice. A dozen men got up to take the call. All were Mr Wong.

Such similarities are certain to cause confusion to the western visitor unfamiliar with the system of Chinese names. You may be introduced to a group of six people, five of whom are named Li. If you ask, innocently, if they are related, the question is likely to raise a polite smile. Their names may be written in different characters so that although the surnames are pronounced the same, the written names are completely different.

It's the same when you go to a factory or an office and meet Mr Cai, the director, and Madame Cai, the sales manager. Don't assume they are married. The characters for their names may be different and, what's more, Madame Cai may be using her own birthname, a common practice in China long before women's liberation made it acceptable in the west.

Names

The comparatively small number of Chinese common family names leads to an imaginative use of given names. Take ours.

Iris Wong writes:

The family name Wong (Wang or Huang in *pinyin*) means descendants of the emperor. The character Po means 'treasured'. Yee means a young child. So my given name, Po-yee, means I am, literally, a Treasured Child.

Like most other Hongkong Chinese of my age, I also have an English given name. I was named Iris the first day I went to an English-speaking Catholic school where the teacher called us one by one to her desk and asked if we had a foreign name.

What letter of the alphabet did I like most? I nominated 'I'. She gave me a list of suggested names. I have been Iris ever since.

Sin Lok-gar writes:

There are several ways to get a Chinese name. If you are called Smith, there is a set translation, Si Mat-sze. If you have a name which means something in Chinese, like Bridge, that can be easily translated into a Chinese surname. In this instance, the character Qiao, which means 'bridge'.

In my case, there is a set translation for the name Sinclair. But an old friend of mine helped baptise me in the Chinese manner by putting sounds which fit my name in Cantonese (the language of Hongkong) into characters. Thus I became Sin Lok-gar. In Cantonese, this translates, roughly, as 'to wash in happiness and affluence'. Not a bad name.

Then an old and knowledgeable professor I knew at Zhongshan University in Guangzhou gave me a translation that puts my name into more formal characters. In *pinyin*, this is Xin Ker-lai and the characters mean 'to strive with against difficulties and to come with a good personality'. Also pretty good.

But the Cantonese love playing with words and giving nicknames that reflect a person's traits and habits. So despite my two extremely auspicious formal names, to all my friends in Hongkong I am universally known by my nickname that mirrors my fondness for spicy food. They call me Sin Gar-lai, the curry man.

The Minorities

There are in China at least 80 million people who are classified as being non-Han. They are citizens of the People's Republic with all the rights of anyone else. Indeed, when it comes to such matters as family planning, it can be argued that the minority nationalities often have considerably more rights than others. They are not held so strictly to the one-child rule.

Most of the people who make up the 56 recognised minority tribes and races live in the outer ring of China. This is an enormous arc that sweeps from the plains of Manchuria, through the broad steppes of Mongolia and the Ordes, over the deserts of Xinjiang and down through the ice plateau of Tibet and Qinghai into the shrouded rain mountains of Yunnan and Guangxi.

The minorities are in many ways privileged. This aged Miao grandfather up in his mountaintop home in Guizhou is making a bamboo flute for his family.

Many live in the rich heartlands of China along with Han neighbours, but most occupy the outer areas, beyond the Great Wall in the north, in the deserts of the west and in the jungles and mountains of the south.

Among these minority races there is diversity of astonishing variety. There are racial Koreans and Mongols, Turks, Kazaks, Russians, Tartars and Thais. Counted among the minorities are the 7.5 million Hui, mostly racial Han but whose generations-long devotion to Islam has made them a special group who have their own autonomous province of Ningxia. Biggest of the nationalities are the Zhuang, 14 million of them who largely rule themselves in the beautiful southern province of Guangxi. In Yunnan, there is an incredible racial hodgepodge in the mountains with more than 23 racial minorities living in harmony amid the hilly valleys.

In the mountainous province of Guizhou, a natural fortress largely impenetrable until this century, there are five million Miao; their racial cousins in Laos and Vietnam have been largely exterminated by modern foes but in China they live on. Sharing Guizhou with them are many other tribes including the two million Bouyei, laughing racial Thais who remained behind when most of their nationality emigrated many centuries ago, in flight from the fury of another minority, the Mongols. The Bouyei still speak Thai.

Other large groups include Dong, Hani, Yao and five million Yi in the southwestern mountains. There are five million Manchus in the northwest, largely assimilated within the overwhelming Han sea, and 2.5 million Mongols. Around their lonely monasteries on the roof of the world, four million Tibetans live much as they have for centuries. All these groups cling to their own languages, customs and religions. Many follow a traditional way of life, like the nomadic Ewenki who hunt the Manchurian forests, or the million Kirghiz herders of Xinjiang.

Under the Chinese constitution, all are guaranteed a degree of self rule. The five stars on the red flag of modern China symbolise the fact that China is not one race, but a collection of peoples. Most casual visitors who go to China on one of the normal tours will be unlikely to meet any of these charming folk. But if you should stray into the tribal areas and spot people who dress differently from the average Chinese, the chances are they are one of the many minorities.

North versus South

Even among the vast family of the Han, there is much diversity. Travelling from Beijing to Guangzhou, one can see the peoples change. The further south you go, the lighter, more delicate, finer-featured, tend to be the people. Of course, this is painting the racial picture with very broad brushstrokes and talking in huge generalities. Basically, however, it's true.

Any anthropologist will tell you the Han people developed on the great curve of the Huanghe somewhere around the present-day borders of Henan and Shanxi. As the population grew, there was pressure to increase the area occupied by the tribe, the dukedoms, the kingdoms and the empire. To the north, there were the wild lands inhabited by the savage nomads. To the west lay uncertain deserts and to the east the sea. So the Han tended to drift south to occupy empty lands and then into areas inhabited by a colourful montage of many other tribes and races.

Going through Henan and neighbouring provinces today, the photographer's eye is drawn magnetically to those seamed, hardy peasant faces, wonderfully photogenic. These are the racial core of the Han and 2000 years ago, most 'Chinese' would have looked like this. But as the eternal pressure of an ever-increasing population forced the boundaries of settlement inexorably towards the south, the Han met, fought, conquered, married and bred with many other races. All were absorbed into the growing Chinese family. Thus the Cantonese, for example, are now a distinctive type of people descended from the Northerners. They are Han, of course, but few can argue that they are a different variety of Han from the people who inhabit ancient ancestral homelands like Hebei or Shaanxi.

Compare China with Europe. The 'Europeans' occupied that continent in waves, most of which originated in Asia. (The Finns and Hungarians are both descended from the Huns. The Turks came from present-day Xinjiang. The Tartars who ruled Russia and Poland for centuries are Mongols.) Going from Scandinavia to Sicily, the peoples change. It is similar in China. Just as not all Scandinavians are the picture postcard tall, blonde, blue-eyed Aryan, neither are Northern Chinese the bulky, stolid type pictured as Han. Similarly, in the south, there are many large, stocky Cantonese. There is enough truth in the general stereotype, however, to make the generalities worthwhile.

The Dividing Line

North and south are normally separated by the line of the Yangzi. For most purposes, this is accurate enough. Settlement of the vast, rich Yangzi Valley marked an era of huge expansion for the Han. Then they moved on into the vibrant racial stewpot of the south and southwest where myriad tribes of different races were encountered. Some remained aloof and today are still distinctive minority races (the Miao of Guizhou and the Yao of Yunnan) while others blended with and married into the Han, disappearing as separate racial entities. In similar fashion, races have been absorbed in Europe by conquering nations. Where now are the Picts of Scotland?

The Hua Qiao

Some of the most important people in China, economically, are not there at all. These are the Overseas Chinese, the sojourners, the vastly wealthy communities which have sprung up far from the ancestral shores. There are, according to varying estimates, between 30 million and 54 million of them, depending on how you count.

Although the Hua Qiao do not live in China, they are an integral and vital part of the national economy. It is they who have provided much of the financial fuel which has powered the country towards industrialisation. Back in their ancestral villages, the more successful of these long-gone sons are venerated like living gods. In the vicinity of Chaozhou in Eastern Guangdong, the name Li Kashing, the mighty mega-tycoon of Hongkong, is spoken of with awe. Little wonder; a university that any country would be proud of has been built with his largess. Hospitals, clinics, old folks' homes, schools, temples, libraries and parks bear his name.

The Shantou region, from where Li and so many other successful Chinese hail, has a population of 10 million. Official counts put the Overseas Chinese population who can trace their roots to this tiny area at a similar total. They are centred in Thailand, Hongkong and America.

The town of Toishan in the Pearl delta has 800,000 souls. In California, there are also 800,000 Toishan folk, many of them fourth generation Americans. They include the eminent American

Chinese artist Dong Kingman who in 1987 made a sentimental journey home after more than six decades.

Thailand has at least eight million ethnic Chinese. The six million Hongkongers are 98 per cent Chinese. The Philippines has three million, Indonesia has an unknown number, depending on whether you count Chinese by their birthplace or their ancient racial heritage. The people of bustling Singapore are 75 per cent Chinese and in Malaysia, 35 per cent of the folk are of Chinese descent. In Calgary, on the wide Canadian prairies, there are 42,000 Chinese. Lima in Peru has three Cantonese-language radio stations and there are Chinese daily newspapers in Sydney and Melbourne. In Tahiti, 10 per cent of the people are Chinese. And there are growing Chinatowns throughout the world from Amsterdam to Seattle.

No matter how long they have been away, a few years or 1000 years like the Chinese of southern Borneo, they still feel their ties to the ancestral villages. Money pours back home. Sojourners from the Sai Yap (Four Counties) area of the Pearl River delta have flooded that rich plain with donations, bequests and investments to make it the richest area of all China. The Shanghai textile barons of Hongkong have put some of their profits back home into new factories on the Huangpu River.

In return for this largess, areas with sizeable communal links overseas maintain large and efficient offices to cater to the Hua Qiao when they make visits home. 'Overseas Chinese' hotels featuring local culinary delights are reserved for them.

And in places like Sai Yap, every town houses a genealogical detective office to trace back the roots of families which may have left four generations earlier to go to Kam Shan (Golden Mountain —California) to dig for gold or build railways.

If a gangly young American comes to town with only the vaguest knowledge of where his great-great-grandfather hailed from, local experts can track down his native hamlet and introduce him to his distant relatives who remained behind.

Chapter Three

CHINA LANDSCAPE

All the rivers flow into the sea
And yet the sea is not full.

To talk about China as a country is like referring to Europe as a single nation. Except China is a lot bigger, has three times as many people and in many ways is arguably more complex as a society.

Confronting outsiders, Chinese tend to form a united front. Within the homeland, they divide swiftly into provincial and local groupings. Just as a travelling American abroad will identify himself as being from Portland, Oregon, or Houston, Texas, so will a Chinese proclaim himself from Zhejiang province or Jiangsu.

If he is meeting a compatriot from the same province, he will identify himself more locally. If he hails from Guangdong and meets a fellow Cantonese, he will identify himself by county or region. Then village. Then clan. Local pride is intense; Chinese blood is a lot thicker than the muddy waters of the Yellow River.

The vast size and population of China makes generalities difficult, if not meaningless.

Guangdong province, for instance, has 66 million people who speak their own distinctive dialect (with many diverse internal strains within the provincial boundaries). It is as big as Kansas and has 27 times as many people. Sichuan province, out in its France-sized mountain-guarded basin at the headwaters of the Yangzi, contains more people than the combined populations of Canada, Australia, New Zealand, Malaysia, Austria, Guatemala, Holland, Portugal and Greece. Xinjiang, which has a mere 12 million people, is larger than all Western Europe. The bulk of the people are Muslim Uygurs who speak old Turkish, basically understandable even today to a resident of Istanbul.

How can one compare living conditions in humid, tropical Hainan Island with those in the frigid tundra forests of northern Heilongjiang? From the Wusuli River in Manchuria to the rice paddies of Hainan is as great a distance as from London to the banks of the River Niger or from New York to Peru.

The climatic differences alone make for gulfs in the lifestyles; while tourists are splashing beneath the coconut palms on the beaches around Sanya in January, it can be 25 degrees below zero in Mongolia where the Siberian winds moan over the northern steppes.

The Land

China is the world's third largest country (after the Soviet Union and the United States). It covers 9.6 million square kilometres. It runs 5500 kilometres from the tropical sand dunes of Nansha Islands, four degrees north of the equator in the South China Sea, to the frigid banks of the Black Dragon River. When the sun rises over Shanghai, dawn is still four hours away in Kashgar, 5200 kilometres to the west.

Along her 20,000 kilometres of land boundaries, the People's Liberation Army, biggest in the world with four million soldiers, stands watch over 13 neighbouring countries and territories. Some neighbours are friendly; others are not. They are Korea, Hongkong, Vietnam, Laos, Burma, India, Bhutan, Sikkim, Nepal, Pakistan, Afghanistan, the Soviet Union and Outer Mongolia. Across the seas, Japan, the Philippines, Brunei, Malaysia and Indonesia have all had historic trade links with China going back well over 1000 years.

Indeed, from the viewpoint of a mandarin at the imperial court in Kaifeng during the Tang Dynasty, China was justifiably the Middle Kingdom.

Face of the Land

The common image of China in the west is a land of endless rice paddies with patient peasants plodding along behind equally placid water buffaloes. In large part, this likeness is astonishingly accurate. Such sights can be seen anywhere in the Yangzi valley and the fertile ricelands of the south. But two-thirds of China's 9.6 million square kilometres are hills, mountains and plateaux. The highest peak is Qomolangma (Mount Everest) at 8848 metres, one of 100 cloud-piercers more than 7000 metres in height.

Geographers describe China as a land of three giant steps. The lowest is the arc that faces the seas, the fertile crescent in which the bulk of the people live. Further inland, a giant step goes upwards to the inland ranges from Yunnan and Guizhou to the loess highlands and the Mongolian steppes. The top step is the high, icy Tibet-Qinghai plateau and the enormous mountains that gird the roof of the world.

The Coast

From the mouth of the Yalu River on the Korean border down to where the Beilun River separates China from Vietnam, there are 18,000 kilometres of coastline. Offshore, the two major islands of Hainan and Taiwan are the largest of many thousands of islands.

Decent deepwater harbours are surprisingly few. The best on the entire coast is the island-girded waters of Fragrant Harbour, Hongkong. Others are Dalian, Qindao and Tianjin, which serve Beijing and the northern provinces, the enormous anchorages that line the Huangpu River at Shanghai, and the beautiful little snug ports of Wenzhou, Xiamen and Shantou on the jagged southeastern coastal fringe. Up the Pearl River is Guangzhou, the historic old gateway to China, and further down the coast is the oil city port of Zhanjiang.

The Rivers

For thousands of years, peasants have called the Huanghe (Yellow River) by a name that is sadly appropriate. 'China's Sorrow' is how they refer to the silt-choked waters of the river which nurtured the earliest Chinese civilisation. On its 5464 kilometre journey down from the ice plateau of Qinghai province, the Huanghe picks up an incredible load of silt. This is carried with the flood as it rushes down from the mountains and through the loess lands to the broad North China Plain. There, the river slows down as it meanders towards the Gulf of Bohai. When the waters slow, the silt drops to the river bed. Over millions of years the steady deposits of silt have built up the riverbed. Now, it flows high above the level of the surrounding plains. At incredible cost in toil, sweat and expenditure, China's rulers for 5000 years have tried to raise banks to control the river. Until now, none has succeeded. Periodically, melting ice in the highlands and heavy rains in the middle reaches of the river have caused the waters to rise and overflow the banks. The results have historically been heavy death tolls in flooding and even more immense costs in lives and suffering because of starvation in the resulting famines. When the communists took control of China in 1949, one of the first things they instituted was a high-powered Yellow River Conservation Commission. Teams of engineers, hydrologists, land control experts and afforestation workers have since confined the Huanghe within iron and concrete channels eight kilometres wide. For the first time in history, the Yellow River seems genuinely to be under the control of man. It is one of the proudest achievements of Beijing. Despite record rainfalls and cold spells which have frozen the waters solid for more than 100 kilometres—forming dangerous dams of natural ice—the river in recent years has not seriously threatened the scores of millions who live along its lower floodplains.

Even more majestic and certainly more impressive is the Yangzi or Changjiang as it is commonly called in Chinese. The name means 'Long River' and at 6300 kilometres from the gaping 85-kilometre-wide mouth to the headwaters in Tibet and Qinghai, it is certainly apt. It forms a broad, muddy highway from the metropolis of Shanghai that cuts directly into the heart of China. Ships up to 10,000 tons can easily sail 300 kilometres straight up-river to Nanjing.

The Pearl River that flows through the south is one of the friendliest waterways on earth. Ferries, sampans, vessels from every port in the world and fishing fleets of thousands of sailing junks make its busy estuary a delight. It ambles through some of the most scenic areas of China; a tributary, the Li, wends its way through the sugarloaf mountains of Guilin, one of the most famed sights in China. It is also a bustling commercial waterway with many important manufacturing towns clustered along its 2197-kilometre length. Densely populated and the richest area in China, the delta area can be explored by tourists on chugging local ferries or hovercraft that speed at 50 knots from Hongkong to such river ports as Guangzhou, Macau, Jiangmen or 480 kilometres upstream to Wuzhou in Guangxi province.

Cartographers have mapped more than 50,000 rivers and their combined flow of 2,600,000,000,000 million cubic metres gives China hydroelectric power reserves of 680 million kilowatts, largest in the world.

Hot and Cold

It's impossible to summarise the Chinese climate simply because it is so variable over such a huge area. Basically, the north is very cold in winter, the south surprising chilly.

It is one of the oddities of life in China that in winter, you are likely to be steaming, uncomfortably hot in the rigid north while you are shivering, chilled to the bone in the comparatively balmy south.

Here's why ...

It is an act of faith to all Chinese that north of the Yangzi, houses must be kept tightly closed through the winter months. Inside, coal fires burn below clay *kangs* and the temperatures soar. It is the same in tourist hotels where the heat is turned up as high as it can go. Outside, ice bedecks the barren branches of the plane trees and snow lies deep. Inside, it's like a sauna.

Meanwhile, it is an equally held belief that South China never freezes. Just try believing this theory when the winter gales come coursing down from Siberia; in unheated southern concrete buildings, the temperature drops to ice-box levels and three layers of clothes can't keep out the penetrating cold.

Bone-chilling cold in the northern winter, steambath-humid in the south in summer, delightfully pleasant everywhere in autumn, uncertain universally in the spring, the climate of China is as variable as the landscape.

In summer, apart from the highlands, China is hot. There are degrees of discomfort, from the dry, arid heat of the west to the sapping, dripping humidity of the verdant moist southlands.

Chinese old wives' tales say there are four furnace cities in

North China winters can be frigid. Overseas Chinese from tropical climes dress in furs and padded clothes to cope with the chill. But, like this Hongkonger, they say the warmth of visiting the ancestral homeland keeps the cold at bay.

China: Nanchang in Jiangxi, Chongqing in Sichuan, Wuhan in Hubei and Changsha in Hunan. Any visitor to the sauna-like south in the summer can probably nominate a few more.

The Cities

Chinese cities may have been the foundries of civilisation. But in the modern era, many of them are simply vast slums with potholed, undrained streets and dusty, unpaved footpaths between endless dreary blocks of five-storey apartment buildings and factories. Dismal as is the vast suburban sprawl that surrounds most Chinese cities, the visitor must understand that these are signs of progress. With the exception of Shanghai and a handful of other cities, mostly ports, the major towns of China before 1949 were comparatively small. It was the drive towards industrialisation that saw them boom.

Formerly, city folk lived mostly in squat, single-storey brick homes with a small courtyard enclosed by a wall and the main windows facing south to catch the winter sun. In most cities, these have gone or have an imminent appointment with the bulldozers. They are replaced with five-storey buildings depressingly similar from Shenyang to Haikou. Unlovely though they be, these blocks efficiently house huge numbers of people. Families may be squeezed into tiny two- or three-room apartments in conditions which would be intolerable elsewhere by western standards. By Chinese measures, people are deemed fortunate indeed to have such quarters.

In general, the compact central areas of the cities—especially the waterfronts and riverbanks in ports and districts around the railway stations—tend to be the most interesting for visitors. Outside the town centres, industrial and housing blocks march off in a panorama of glum similarity.

One reason that most Chinese cityscapes are the same depressing five- or six-storey buildings with few modern high-rises poking above the squat landscape is the shortage of elevators. It's difficult to live much higher than the sixth floor if one has to use the stairs.

Typical of modern housing throughout the nation, these drab apartment blocks offer modern homes—albeit crowded—to industrial workers.

The Big City

Although 80 per cent of China's population lives in the countryside, this still leaves more than 200 million occupying cities. Shanghai is said to be the biggest city in the world with 12 million people. This is not true. The great port on the Huangpu is big, all right, but it's not that big. Similar misconceptions and misleading statistics apply to many other city populations. This is because of the Chinese way of counting things. As in so many other aspects of life, they do things their way.

In 1984, the Central Government reorganised the political structure of the nation. While the provinces remained the same (Hainan Island was split from Guangdong to become the 30th province in 1988), the internal arrangements were changed. This meant that big chunks of provinces were put into logical regions that could be developed as sensible economic districts.

Take Shantou, in eastern Guangdong. This is the home of the Chaozhou people, a distinctive sub-group of the great Cantonese family. They speak their own language, have their own cuisine, are strongly bonded together. So the Chaozhou area was amalgamated into one region. For some reasons known only to faceless planners in Beijing, these regions were called 'cities'. Thus Shantou 'city' comprises two cities, eight counties, 10,000 square kilometres and 10 million people. The real old port town, a city in the normally accepted sense of the word, has less than two million people.

So when you hear Chinese officials talking of Beijing having eight million people, or Shanghai having a population of 12 million, they are including very extensive areas of the hinterland. It's as though Britain claimed London had 20 million people, toting up the populations of Kent, Middlesex, Surrey and the other home counties. Or if America counted the population of New Jersey, most of Connecticut and a huge swathe of New York State and proclaimed New York city held 25 million souls. Shanghai city, by my guess, has about six million people in the city proper.

In recent years, China has laid great stress on making her old cities more liveable in the era of industrialisation. Foreign experts from many disciplines have taken part in seminars aimed at teaching Chinese planners how to design functional, efficient and attractive towns. Attempts at beautification have been made in a number of cities. In Guangzhou, for instance, the go-ahead administration has planted millions of flowering shrubs and other plants. In the capital, landscaping the dull ochre soil of the northern plains has been tried in attempts to make the city more attractive.

For many western visitors, however, the first and remaining impression of the majority of Chinese cities is of a drab, dreary landscape of endless blocks of dingy, featureless apartments marching off into the polluted haze and divided by bare plots of barren earth.

Beijing

The national capital is one of the great cities of the world. By Chinese standards, it is comparatively modern; it was first used as the imperial capital by Kublai Khan in the 13th century.

Its history goes back a long way before the great Mongol ruler established the seat of the Yuan Dynasty in the city on the dusty North China Plain. According to legend, a city stood near the present Tiananmen Square in 1200 BC. It was the capital of the Kingdom of Yen before it was razed by Qin Shihuang in his campaign to unify China. The invading Kitan Tartars grabbed the city in AD 986 and declared it their capital. Successive armies of conquerers and Chinese regimes swept back and forth over the area for centuries during which the city lived under many banners, and had many names.

The Mongols called it Khanbalik (City of the Khan) and from here ruled their vast domains in China. The Chinese Ming Dynasty moved the seat of imperial rule to Nanjing (which means Southern Capital) for a brief period before moving back to Beijing (Northern Capital) so they could keep a watchful eye on the uneasy nomad borderlands.

When the Qing regime was imposed in 1644, the new rulers were happy to keep Beijing as the imperial capital because it was so close to their ancestral homeland in Manchuria. During their brief tenure in power, the Kuomintang ruled from Nanjing and in that period, Beijing was occupied by the Japanese. With the communist victory in 1949, Mao moved the seat of government back to the old imperial capital.

Shanghai

The huge port city on the Huangpu has character. It's a town of solidly built workers who proudly boast their rowdy heritage in what once gloried in its role as the wickedest city on earth. It is a pup of a city; until greedy westerners seized the place as a treaty port after the first Opium War in 1841, it was a tiny walled town on a mudbank on a forgotten tributary of the Yangzi.

So Shanghailanders trace their roots to other places. They come mostly from the surrounding provinces of Zhejiang and Jiangsu but some look back to ancestral villages in virtually every province in the land. A walk along the Bund takes you on a stroll through an architectural museum; almost all the buildings went up there before the Japanese invasion in 1937 and the occupation of the International Settlement in 1941.

Guangzhou

Exhuberant, noisy, cheerful, smiling, quick to make a dollar, the Cantonese are a jovial bunch. Their long tradition of links with the outside world makes foreigners familiar to them. Almost everyone you meet has a cousin in California, a brother running a restaurant in Manchester or a friend studying computers in Australia.

Vastly proud of its reputation as the culinary capital of China, the locals delight in eating, drinking and making merry. They are also the consumate traders of China, tracing their role as the major gateway to the world back to the Tang Dynasty when Arab dows dropped anchor in the Pearl River.

Xian

Famed for the buried terracotta warriors that guarded the tomb of the Great Unifier, Qin Shihuang, Xian was the capital of a dozen dynasties. A vast museum of the ages, the city has been occupied for many thousands of years, long before the first dynasty. On the outskirts of town, not far from where the Wei River joins the Huanghe on the very spot where many anthropologists believe the first Chinese agronomists farmed, there is the well-preserved remains of a 6000-year-old village.

One of the most popular axis of the tourist schedule, Xian has boomed with tourism in the past decade. The past here is profitable and new hotels—Swedish, German, Hongkong and Swiss are joint venture partners—offer high quality accommodation as a base for exploring dynastic China and its treasures.

Kaifeng-Zhengzhou-Luoyang

This triumvirate of cities in Henan along the Yellow River were all at various times capitals of dukedoms, kingdoms and of all imperial China. Visitors who go to one of these cities are urged strongly not to depart without seeing all three of them. There are frequent inexpensive bus trips between the cities and each has a charm and character of its own. Each also preserves with great enthusiasm the relics of the past that make this area of the Huanghe Valley stake its claim to being the cradle of Chinese civilisation.

Kaifeng was a major staging post on the Silk Route and the family Shih who still live in the town are the last remnants of the practising Judaic Chinese community.

Near Luoyang, at Longmen, are the grottoes carved over a period of seven dynasties where 100,000 figures of Buddha once occupied caves hacked out of the solid rock cliffs. Vandals over the centuries have destroyed most of the figures but thousands, some partly shattered, remain as reminders of a persistent faith.

Not far from Zhengzhou, modern commercial and political capital of Henan, carved stone monuments stand sentinel on lonely hillsides, looking out over rolling loess hills where they guard the graves of Song Dynasty rulers. This area is rich in artefacts, museums, legend and history.

Chongqing

What a dump. The site is scenic enough, set on a spur surrounded on three sides by the Yangzi and a major tributary. But the high steps that allow river craft to rise up the steep flanks as the water level rises and falls with the season are normally covered with filth. The climate is dreadful, usually overcast and smoggy and the town is one big slum. Despite that, it has a certain charm and the historical links are fascinating. It was to this remote town that Chiang Kai-shek and the Nationalists retreated in 1937 in front of the advancing Japanese and it was here that Free China had its capital during the wartime years.

Tianjin

Drab and miserable, the huge northern port has little to recommend it to visitors unless you have a penchant for looking at factories and chimneys belching choking clouds of smoke.

As major entrepot for the Northern Plains, as a huge industrial base and a hub for transport, Tianjin is a vital economic force in China. As a place of interest, it has virtually nothing to offer except boredom and phenomenal pollution.

Wuhan

The capital of Hubei province in the central Yangzi has a population of about 3.5 million. It is a conurbation formed by the three old cities of Hankou, Wuchang and Hanyang, set on the banks where the Han River joins the mighty Yangzi. Wuhan has considerable charm. Although far inland, its history as a major treaty port has given its lively people a cosmopolitan outlook.

Qingdao

What a delight! A lovely city which still largely bears the proud Teutonic architectural stamp put on the harbour promenades by Germany when the city was capital of the Kaiser's colony in China before the Second World War. Old castles that look as though they belong at home alongside the Rhine and sturdy stone cathedrals which appear to have been built to withstand a siege dominate the skyline.

Shandong folk are renowned for their hearty appetites, good humour and capacity for hard work.

Nanning

Very few foreigners ever make it to the southernmost provincial capital in the land. This is a great pity. The sleepy little city on the upper reaches of the Pearl River in Guangxi is a marvellous gem. Girded by clumps of enormous bamboo, the city echoes in the spring to the sound of local Zhuang tribesmen (there are 14 million of them!) singing in their local dialect to attract lovers.

Gracious parks, hotels set amid gardens and broad tree-lined avenues speak of the French heritage which seeped up from Vietnam less than 100 kilometres to the south.

Xiamen

Another favourite city of mine, this wonderful port city in southern Fujian is the homeland of many millions of Overseas Chinese. It is outward looking and has been for well over 1000 years during which the intrepid traders of Amoy (its old name) put out to sea in their junks to the distant savage lands of the south seas. Today, in museums as far distant as Borneo and India, the jars and ornaments they carried as trade goods can be seen.

It is a city of smiles. Wander the narrow, bustling streets and drop into free enterprise restaurants, stop to admire clay teapots or simply go into a restaurant and you will meet friendly folk eager to help.

Hangzhou

Imperial seat of power during the Southern Song Dynasty (when barbarian invaders held sway in the traditional northern capitals), Hangzhou makes the most of its past. For centuries, it was regarded as a cultural citadel where painting, literature, landscape gardening, architecture and drama flourished. Today, local folk like to think much of this rich legacy remains.

The focal point of the town is the scenic West Lake. For at least 800 years, poets have waxed lyrical about this willow-fringed expanse of shallow water, an artificial expanse lined by swept roof pavilions, studded with temple-dotted islands. It's pleasant enough, but hardly one of the great sights of China despite endless enthusing by Hangzhou citizens to whom West Lake is the centre of the universe.

As the terminus of the Silk Road and southern port of the Grand Canal, Hangzhou was once a vital economic hub. It is still an important city for both manufacturing and tourism.

Changsha

The stamp of Chairman Mao is still very much evident in the provincial capital where he spent much of his early life, worked as a teacher and where, so legend has it, he wrote his first thesis 'On Revolution' while sitting in an orange grove on the Xiang River.

Changsha is an interesting place if only for the remembrance of Mao and other revolutionary heroes. The late president of China, Liu Shaochi, was also born near by. In glorious brotherly harmony, Liu was purged by Mao in 1966 and sent down to the countryside to learn from the peasants. He died of cancer of the nose after Comrade Jiang Qing, Mao's wife, forbade doctors to give him treatment.

Nanjing

Capital of China during the Kuomintang era, Nanjing is set on the banks of the Yangzi where the Zijin Shan (Purple and Gold Mountains) meet the river. The venerated father of modern China, Dr Sun Yat-sen, lies in his stately mausoleum atop a magnificent open staircase that climbs Purple Mountain.

The city was the subject of the horrific Rape of Nanjing in 1937 when Japanese soldiers murdered an estimated 300,000 people in one of the most vicious war crimes in history. More people than this, however, were slain when the Taiping rebels took the city in the 1860s and probably just as many were butchered when the Ever Victorious Army of General Charles Gordon reclaimed the city for the Manchu rulers.

Today, Nanjing is a pleasant city of trees and boulevards. One notable feature is the gigantic double-layered bridge crossing the Yangzi, a symbol of Chinese pride and progress.

Place Names

It comes as a disappointment to visitors to find those exotic, romantic names of provinces and towns are, when translated, often boring and as mundane as those back home.

There are, to be sure, places called The Temple of Eternal Enlightenment and The Pond of the Pure White Egret.

But most names are nothing as exciting.

Take some of the provinces. Shandong means Mountain East. Henan means South of the River. Guangdong means Broad East while, logically, the next province up the Xi (West) River is Guangxi which means Broad West. Sichuan means Four Rivers, because that's where four rivers join to form the broad Yangzi, the real name of which is—boring!—Changjiang or Long River.

Yunnan means Beneath the Clouds because of the misty weather.

The three Manchurian provinces are known collectively as Dong Bei, the Northeast. Thankfully, the most northern one of all has an exotic name, Heilongjiang, which means Black Dragon River.

Ask your tour guide or hotel staff for the name of the city and province and what the characters mean in English. They will be happy to tell you. Then ask them for the other, unofficial names of local places. These are almost invariably more interesting.

Guangzhou, for example, means Broad City. Terrific. Much more romantic is the legend of how the place was founded by five fairies who rode into town on five goats. The fairies flew off but the goats remain in the form of an imposing statue in the city's Yue Xie Park. The legend is the basis for Old Canton being known to locals as The City of the Five Rams. Most other towns and cities have similar stories and local folk will delight in explaining them to you.

Chapter Four

BELIEFS

When men are sincere, the gods are moved and they answer.

Accept your destiny, as you do your duty,
Be satisfied with your position
And obey the voice of heaven.

A few years ago, I was with a party of foreign diplomats based in Hongkong who were being escorted around Zhejiang province by senior officials. Wandering away from the group, a Hongkong friend and I found ourselves in a small village. The locals were typically friendly and asked us into their homes for tea.

Looking around, we saw there was one big building in the village, a modern structure built like a large barn. Inside, we found more than 100 women and girls working at a furious pace. They were making gods.

'What you're looking at here,' my wise old companion commented, 'is the biggest growth industry in China.

'Religion is on the way back.'

How right he was.

Plenty of Choices

When it comes to choosing a religion, the Chinese have a multitude of choices. There are all those available to the western world and a variety of home-grown selections as well. Officially, China is a secular state. The constitution (revised numerous times since 1949) guarantees freedom of religion.

A Chinese can quite happily mix up a cocktail of religions. He can believe in Buddha, follow the preachings of the philosopher Confucius, hold precious The Way of Taoism and also without qualms attend Christian services. Is this hypocrisy, as some westerners contend, or more charitably a broad outlook which takes the best aspects of all possible faiths? Or is it a multi-choice bet that covers all eventualities that guarantees backing a winner in the religious wagers? Take your pick.

If the visitor asks a modern Chinese, bluntly: 'What is your religion?' the answer is likely to be a confused silence. The most common answer is probably 'None.' At home, however, there will be ancestral portraits on the wall, hinting at a Confucian-like regard for the ancestors, and incense may burn in front of a family altar which also contains the likenesses of traditional deities.

Over the centuries, China has warmly accepted religious infusions from abroad. The basic faith of the people, however, has remained with the two codes of ethical conduct developed in China itself,

Taoism and the teachings of Confucius, wedded to the imported religion of Buddhism which came over the Himalayas from India and greatly affected China during the Tang Dynasty.

Interwoven, intermixed and mingled richly, the three beliefs have borrowed so extensively from each other it is now difficult to know where one religion ends and another faith begins. In practice, Taoism-Confucianism-Buddhism in China is one vast body of faith. There are no contradictions in finding Taoists praying in Buddhist temples and vice versa. The great underlying faith of all Chinese beliefs, and one that transcends all religions, is the most ancient practice of all, ancestor worship.

The Party

In practice, the state religion is orthodox communism, Marxist-Leninism with the addition of China's own Maoist legacy. This version of perceived truth has now been leavened with The Word As Spoken By Deng Xiaoping which has made the economic teachings of the Great Helmsman more realistic.

The Party has 47 million members, give or take a million. The figure is always changing as unpopular figures are dumped, the corrupt are weeded out or a new batch of upwardly-mobile Chutties (Communist Urban Technocrats) join the ranks of the Party faithful. Belief in the infallibility of the sainted Karl Marx, the preachings of the apostle Vladimir Ilyich Lenin or the practices of Comrade Deng are not really necessary for membership. Young Chinese join the Party for the same reasons an accountant in Manchester joins the Jaycees or a Chicago draper joins Rotary—it's a way to make contacts and get ahead in life.

Still, the Party has a kernel of True Believers who see the teachings of Marx as the broad highway towards a better and more equitable future for all.

The Great Teacher

It is impossible to over-emphasise the importance of Confucius to Chinese civilisation. The imprint of the sage has been stamped firmly on the way of life of the nation for 24 centuries. The habits and customs of Chinese daily life today still sway to the teachings of the philosopher who laid down the precepts of filial piety, obedience and duty.

Kung Fuzi was born in Qufu in Shandong province in 551 BC. His father died when he was young, his mother when the boy was a teenager and he grew up working 'at many despised callings'. As a teacher and a bureaucrat in local dukedoms, Master Kung developed an outlook on life which he taught to a number of disciples. He tossed out old ideas on the supernatural, so popular in peasant worship at the time, and introduced precepts of ethics and man's role in society. The stratified kinship relations and loyalties he outlined were adopted by government and scholars who, even if they did not follow his teachings, largely paid public lip service to them.

Master Kung's code forms the basis of modern Chinese moral

Behind an urn of smouldering incense sticks taking messages to a variety of gods, a young monk looks towards an uncertain future.

outlook and in particular underlies that strong foundation of Chinese society through the ages, the extended family.

The Way

Just as 'Chinese' a faith as the philosophy of Confucius is the great body of ethical belief known as Taoism or The Way. Taoism is based largely on the teachings of the sage Lao Tzu who was born around six centuries before the Christian era. The Way stresses the mystical side of humanity. In return for faith in its precepts, it promises followers immortality. 'Believe, therefore you are,' is the message.

With adherents in Overseas Chinese communities and in the United States and Australia led by the Reverend Timothy Yau of the Ching Chung Temple in Hongkong, it is possible there are now more active followers of the body of beliefs that make up Taoism abroad than there are in China. One reason for this is that Taoist priests were subject to special brutality by the rampaging Guards.

Taoism is built on a practical application of alchemy and medical science and an insistence on vegetarian food, a healthy lifestyle and a general code of conduct that stresses generosity of spirit and comradeship, which has helped promote modern interest in the faith.

Buddhism

The Gautama Buddha lived in Northern India about the same time Confucius taught in Shandong. It took five centuries, however, for the Mahayana sect of Buddhism to transverse the Roof of the World and to be widely accepted in China. Over the centuries, the religion had undergone substantial changes and to all intents was a 'new' religion in China, distinct from the version of Buddhism practised in India. The image of the Buddha is enthroned in giant cliff paintings in many parts of the nation. He stares down with benign faith over the headwaters of the Yangzi, the Yellow River and the Pearl. His golden image can be found in temples in every province and his bland, all-seeing countenance is worshipped by young and old, male and female, Chinese resident and truth-seeker from abroad. Clouds of incense rise in shrines rebuilt in every corner of the country.

The contemplative 'Chan' form of Buddhism stressed meditation and withdrawal from the earthly life. From China, it passed over the Eastern Seas to barbarous Japan where it civilised the unruly islanders and became known as Zen. Split into myriad sects, following an array of local abbots and teachers, the religion took numerous forms. One that developed in the Shaolin monastery on a mountain in Shanxi saw those quiet monks developing a form of self-defence aimed at protecting the unarmed wandering holy men from bandits. Thus was born *kung fu* fighting. Another form of the faith is still practised in religious fervour by Tibetans who hold that their self-exiled ruler, the Dalai Lama, is a living god and a reincarnation of Buddha.

Christianity

Marco Polo never tried to convert his Mongol hosts to his Catholic faith. Other Europeans were not so retiring. In the Ming Dynasty, Portuguese priests, many of them fanatical Jesuits, made enormous efforts to convert the Son of Heaven and senior officials. They strove largely in vain; the court wanted elegant European time-pieces, which were a curiosity of the time, but had little desire for a religion which preached all men were equal.

It wasn't until the 19th century that Christians began to successfully penetrate China. Just as trade was forced on a reluctant regime and nation by the gunship treaties that ended the Opium War, so did the cross get carried into China by missionaries who swept in on the coat-tails of the merchants.

From America, Britain, Germany, Italy, France and Scandinavia, keen young men and women swarmed into the country. First they set up their churches in the coastal ports, then began to seep ever further inland. There was great competition for souls between dour Scots Calvinists and energetic Boston Baptists. The competing claims for holiness by various Protestant sects and Catholics led to a race for souls that saw confused Chinese converts selling out to the highest bidder. Desperate to get their children educated and to fill their bowls in time of famine, so-called Rice Christians were attracted to the altars more by payments of food and aid in this life than promises of eternity in the hereafter. The missionaries did not only preach; they probably attracted more people to their faiths through the many thousands of schools, hospitals and universities they established and ran in China. All were taken over by the state after 1949 and missionaries were thrown out of the country. A few are now permitted back but by and large the government remains distrustful of them and suspicious of their motives.

Those Chinese who did forsake ancient ways to follow Christianity often paid dearly for it. They were despised targets in the Boxer Uprising when many were slaughtered and were again favoured victims in the Cultural Revolution. Despite cynical western claims that Christianity never really got anywhere in China, churches across the land are today attracting record numbers of adherents, including a surprising percentage of young people.

Islam

Up in the north and, certainly, in Xinjiang, people will proudly assert their belief in the One True Faith. In Ningxia, officially an autonomous region for Muslims, mosques dominate the skyline. The call to prayer echoes loudly in many surrounding provinces. There are Islamic communities in every large city.

Islam came early to China, travelling over the Silk Road routes from its birthplace in Arabia. In addition to the many millions of northern minorities who profess the faith, there are an estimated eight million Han Chinese converts. Known as Hui, they are now themselves classified as a national minority and given the right to govern themselves in Ningxia according to the laws of Islam.

Deities

The Chinese heavens must be bursting at the seams with assorted gods, deities, mystical figures, demons, Venerable Celestial Beings, saintly apostles and legendary folk heroes. Scholars contend that there has never been a complete count of this multitude of holy

Putting new faces on ancient gods, these designers at the famed Shiwan pottery kiln at Foshan in Guangdong have brought artistic flair to ancient disciplines. The Old Dragon kiln has been lit for nine centuries and still specialises in making images of the senior 18 deities who followed Buddha.

figures. If there was, it could well compete in sheer numbers with the massive 1982 census of China itself which toted up the billion people of the nation.

Figures of worship abound in China. Traditionally, visitors would see them when they first approached a home. Ferocious scowling door gods stand in proud menace on either side of the entrance to guard those within. Inside, there would be a shrine where ancestors (themselves nearing the stature of respected saintliness) share honours in front of the smouldering incense sticks with local deities and such all-powerful figures as Guan Di, the God of War.

It was the ancestors, in the traditional belief in which Taoism merged with Buddhism, through which the common folk approached the more senior deities of faith and folklore. The departed male patriarchs occupied the top rung on the hierarchical totem pole (as they had done in life) but women frequently sought the aid of an ancestress, particularly in prayers for a son.

Many scholars have pointed out that the traditional Chinese view of heaven coincided with the earthly empires of the dynasties. When the emperor went to the Temple of Heaven in Beijing twice yearly to pray for crops and tranquillity, his messages were directed to Yudi, the Supreme Being. Yudi dealt only with the earthly emperor. His wife, Xi Wang Mu, the earth mother of antiquity, dealt with women's affairs and there was an entire celestial cabinet and bureaucracy staffed by multitudes of lesser gods, deputy deities, assistant August Personages and mandarins of heaven to deal with the prayers of other mortals and their affairs.

In this sprawling bureaucracy of immortals (which has an uncanny resemblance to the creaky over-manned public service of today) demi-gods and deities elbowed each other for responsibility. There were divine figures charged with looking after the kitchen, others with responsibility for the bedroom (a Lord and Lady of the Bedchamber, naturally) and the divine of the latrine.

Many of these gods can be traced back to humans whose valour, honesty, courage or feats of incredible strength or cunning made them famous in their lifetime, elevated them to legendary stature after death and then promoted them to the status of god or goddess. Such a one was Zai Chen. He lived around 1100 BC, a hermit who lived in the mountains, could cast miraculous spells while he rode around on a tiger. He fought for Duke Wu, founder of the Zhou Dynasty, to help overthrow the Shang. After his death (he was supposedly slain by a rival sorcerer) Zai Chen became a god. Today, his gilded figure is a familiar one; as God of Wealth he is one of the most revered and respected of the deities and the object of countless incense sticks and prayers. Likewise venerated are the three Gods of Happiness, jolly old souls who concentrate on spreading satisfaction.

Not surprisingly, the warlike Manchus were extremely partial to Guan Di, God of War. This fearsome, burly and bearded figure must have seemed tailor-made for them. They built more than 1600 shrines in his honour in every corner of the land and he is today not only still venerated as the deity in charge of war but also bears responsibility for detectives. Thus, even in sophisticated Chinese societies, he is honoured still. In Hongkong, when detectives are faced with a difficult crime poser, they burn offerings to the Guan Di shrine in every station, offer him fat roast pork and sweet wine and kowtow in deep respect. When the crime is solved, as often happens, they return to give thanks.

Missionaries

The western idea of missionaries in China, largely sponsored by media-created romances, is of a brave white man or woman penetrating into an ignorant, disease-ridden and dangerous environment to spread one or another of the branches of the Christian faith and to bring sweetness, justice and light to uncouth and ill-educated savages. Needless to say, this notion is not one commonly shared by the Chinese.

The communist view of missionaries is a perception of unwanted crafty, snide foreign intruders who forced their way into the country under the unwelcome protection of gunboats to subvert traditional Chinese values, to undermine the way of life and to slyly implant perverted alien ideas. There is some truth on both sides.

Although a few exceptions have been made and an increasing number of religious figures have been permitted to enter and work in China in recent years, there are still deep suspicions harboured about missionaries. The great bulk of them were hounded out of their parishes and forced out of China in 1950 and there is no way a new generation is going to be allowed back.

The fact that leading converts (to Methodism) included Generalissimo Chiang Kai-shek, his widely detested wife and many other strident anti-communists who fled to Taiwan in 1949 merely reinforces these suspicions.

Many westerners, notably Americans, seem to cling to the idea that they have a God-given, inalienable right to enter China and go where they wish preaching their religion and seeking converts. The fact that they are not allowed to freely do so angers them intensely. They consider it monstrous that the atheistic communist state should be permitted to restrain them.

But have a look at the other side of the coin. What would be the reaction of good Southern Baptists in Alabama or Arkansas if cadres of the Chinese Communist Party were to go traipsing through the Bible Belt distributing copies of *Thoughts of Chairman Mao* and urging the rural populace to rise in revolution? Can one imagine the screams of outrage if True Believers of the Party demanded the freedom to spread their doctrine in America with the same insistence that Christian missionaries press for the 'right' to proselytise in China? Just as the American Congress and people would resist the presence of Chinese communists spreading foreign political theories in their nation, so the Chinese leadership thinks it repugnant for aliens to demand to preach foreign ideas in China.

No way, padre.

Persecution

Religion was one of the prime targets of the Cultural Revolution. Foreign beliefs, Christianity in particular, were seen to be alien, hostile to communism and evil forces to be rooted out. There was dreadful persecution of all religions and any expression of belief was likely to provoke attack by fanatical Red Guards to whom Mao was akin to a god. Tens of thousands of people were slain because of their religious affiliations. Catholic priests accused of espionage were held in jails in solitary confinement for more than a decade.

BELIEFS

A young novice monk at the temple on sacred Putao Shan contemplates a life of meditation. Young people are heading back to the ancient faiths despite official disapproval. The abbot and monks here suffered dreadfully at the hands of the Red Guards.

In these more relaxed times, people are more likely to confess to being Christians, Muslims or Buddhists. Major Christian churches are now open in most large cities and masses in newly-reopened cathedrals as far distant as Guangzhou and Taiyuan draw big followings.

The Red Guards' frenzy—itself a perverted form of religious mania—saw hordes of screaming young vandals burn and smash countless temples, churches, mosques and religious shrines. The cultural destruction was enormous.

With the swing of the political pendulum back towards sanity, the sacred places are being rebuilt, often with funds donated by generous Overseas Chinese who were appalled by the horrific toll taken of the national heritage.

At sacred Putao Shan island, one of the four most revered religious mountains in China, huge amounts of money from Singapore has been funnelled into reconstructing the vast temple. The abbot, who survived vigorous prosecution, told me how boatloads of Red Guards would descend on the island during the Ten Black Years. They went to the peaceful Zhou Shan archipelago on ferries commandeered in Ningbo, Shanghai and other ports, swarmed over the island in joyful chaos, singing Maoist anthems as they ripped down the carved temple doors, smashed ancient stone pillars and crashed the mighty bronze temple bells to the flagstones that had for centuries marked the spots where Buddhists bent in prayer. Many of the monks dragged off for punishment were never seen again. By the mid-1980s, a few survivors had drifted back to Putao Shan and, amazingly, another generation of young men and women had shaved their heads and entered into the devotions of a life of contemplation.

Temples

Feel free to take photographs in temples. There are no restrictions. People do not usually mind you snapping them when they are lighting joss sticks or praying. I usually smile, lift my camera and look at them enquiringly. Almost always, they smile back and nod. It's safe to work on the assumption that you can take pictures in any religious setting. Go ahead and click away. If for some reason there is a ban, some busybody bureaucrat will soon bustle up and stop you. When in doubt, shoot. Many big temples have souvenir shops attached where you can buy statues or prints of local gods.

In mosques, take off your shoes before entering. In other temples, which are common meeting places for a chat and a part of village life, don't bother. But remember, everywhere, that no matter how casual may be the general approach to temples, you are in a place of worship and should show respect and restraint.

Feng Shui

Central to many Chinese religious beliefs is a strong faith in *feng shui*. The words mean, simply, wind and water, and they tie together a package of folklore that can be traced back to before the birth of Chinese civilisation. Even among modern sophisticates, faith in geomancy is total. No Chinese would dream of building a house on the 'eye of a dragon' and almost all good fortune and bad luck can be traced back to benign or baleful effects of *feng shui*.

What does it mean? If you've got one or two years to sit and listen patiently, some aged sage can explain the intricacies of *feng shui* and how it influences your daily life, your bodily functions, your health, marriage, career and business. It rules your existence, dominates your life, guides your destiny. No Chinese would dream of changing the furniture in his office, no land developer would contemplate siting a building, without consulting the *feng shui* man to seek his guidance.

Based on the notion that man and nature have to exist in harmony, closely related to the concept of the *yin* and *yang* of balanced forces of every aspect of existence, *feng shui* is an entire school of environmental and cultural doctrines. Adherents firmly believe spiritual forces inhabit every spot on earth. They influence, for better or worse and for eternity, the fate of people who live there or pass by.

Hills represent dragons. To build a house on the eye of the dragon, thereby irritating the mythical beast, would obviously be hazardous. Therefore, before a new structure goes up, the *feng shui* man must be consulted to ensure it is sited in the most beneficial spot, facing the direction which reaps the most ample harvest in tranquillity and harmony with the elements. *Feng shui* men (and, rarely, women) are figures held in considerable respect in the business community and in awe by villagers.

The effect of wind and water on a building and its inhabitants can be harmful or beneficial, depending on how these influences are channelled. Hence the strategic placement of a mirror on the eave of a house can divert or reflect bad spirits. Doors in a house should never be in a straight line; that would allow evil influences to flow straight into the heart of a mansion. No, sturdy obstacles must be placed in their paths.

The laws of *feng shui* are myriad. How should your desk be placed in the office? Should it be situated so your back is to the window? The *feng shui* man will come, contemplate, study the way in which the fortunes, potentially good, perhaps threatening, look into the room. Then he will make a considered judgement. He will collect a not insignificant fee.

The forces of nature can be greatly beneficial or grossly dangerous. It all depends on how you harness the *feng shui* and channel it to your advantage. Good spirits must be encouraged. Bad demons must be placated. The elements can be encouraged to do both. Indeed, evil geomancers can be hired to plot to harm people blessed with a good *feng shui*.

During the Ming Dynasty, for instance, the city of Chaozhou in Guangdong reached peaks of spectacular prosperity. Its sons became wealthy in business and bright young men succeeded in the imperial civil service examinations for selection as mandarins. Jealous rival towns suspected Chaozhou's good fortune was caused by the marvellous *feng shui*. So they hired an unscrupulous *feng shui* expert to sabotage the wind and water which flowed so advantageously. The geomancer spied out the land. There was one significant hill in the area that he pronounced as holding a candle spirit. To put out the candle, he advised the enemies of Chaozhou to dig a well on the crest of the hill. They did so and sat back eagerly to await the decline and fall of Chaozhou. To their baffled rage, the city soared to even greater heights of power and riches. The *feng shui* man had made a mistake; the hill held not a candle spirit but the essence of a lotus. Instead of quenching a candle, the well merely irrigated the water-hungry lotus spirit, bringing even better good fortune to the town.

Herbal Medicine

Closely associated with the notion of *feng shui* is Chinese herbal medicine and implicit belief in its efficacy. Modern scientific research at medical institutes throughout the world show many of the old herbal potions have a strong chemical base that is replicated in western drugs. For instance, out in the jungles of Guangxi, tribal folk still roam the mountains to collect wild nuts off vines high in the ceiling of the rainforest. These nuts are dried, then ground into powder which is said to aid rheumatism. Current research at the Chinese University of Hongkong's medical school shows the nuts have a strong concentration of the same compound which western scientists prescribe for rheumatic treatment. Chinese herbal doctors have been administering it for well over 1000 years.

There are many similar examples where herbal remedies contain chemicals known to modern science. Such cures were devised in rural China by trial and error over many centuries. During that time, millions of peasants must have been used as guinea pigs by untrained herbalists who administered homemade potions and hoped for the best. If the patients survived, the cure was judged a success. By such means, a vast body of knowledge has been built up and today, in many parts of China, herbal homeopathic cures are frequently used alongside western-style medicine.

Acupuncture

The idea that ills could be cured by sticking pins into people was at first regarded as outrageously bizarre by sceptical westerners. Today, acupuncture clinics can be found throughout the world. This ancient discipline holds that the careful placement of small pins in strategic locations of the human geography influences how the body reacts to stress and internal forces. It has been likened to a form of *feng shui* of the human body. There can be no doubt that it works. In many Chinese hospitals, major surgery is conducted with only a couple of acupuncture injections to cut off feeling to the part of the body that is going under the knife. Worry not; any foreigner undergoing an operation will receive western anaesthetic.

Cutting the Demons' Tail

If you should be driving in China, be eternally on the alert for pedestrians, particularly old folk, who suddenly leap in front of your car. If you miss them by six inches or so as they hurl themselves across your path, this will be great good fortune. You will have cut off the string of demons which follow folk about and the lost band of bad spirits, having been cut off from the nimble pedestrian, are now firmly stuck on your tail. Tough luck. Bad joss.

Festivals

Visitors will find it difficult to discover in advance when religious festivals are being held. Ask friends or hotel staff if any special event is happening in the next few days. They'll probably know but haven't bothered to tell you because it would never occur to them that you could possibly be interested.

If you should be in some suburb or town and see a crowd of

69

people in festive mood, follow them and join in. They'll make you welcome and there's sure to be someone who can tell you in broken English what's going on.

Lunar New Year

The greatest festival is the Lunar New Year. All China closes down for these three days in January or February (depending on how the moon rises) to mark the start of another cycle.

Animal Years

Based on beliefs linked closely with the body of common religion and philosophy, this endless pattern of the years flows smoothly on. Just as some westerners believe in astrological signs, so do many Chinese pay at least lip service to the idea that they are born with qualities belonging to the animal year into which they were born.

Most Americans would not like to be a rat. Chinese born in that year, however, are held to be smart, cunning, brave and clever. The horse year child is expected to have stamina, the snake to exhibit sagacity, the ram to show good business judgement. Just as rival western palm readers may have different opinions about one person, so Chinese soothsayers can attribute various qualities to those born in the same year. You pays your money, you takes your choice.

For the Ancestors

Most major religious festivals in China are officially ignored, based as they are on old religious or philosophical beliefs. They are widely practised by the people, especially in the countryside.

If you should be in a rural area in spring and see hordes of people heading for grave-speckled hillsides, they are carrying oranges and other offerings to their ancestors. The living will sweep the graves of the dead, tidy up the tombs and pay their respects. There is a similar rite in autumn. As winter nears, you may see old ladies lighting bonfires in the streets. This is the festival of the hungry ghosts and they are burning paper gifts to appease the uneasy spirits who may otherwise return to make trouble.

Feast Days

Just as ardent Catholics find a saint to pray to every day, so can Chinese always clutch an excuse for a festival from among their wide collection of deities. Similarly, devotees normally pay homage to their special deities on their feast days, anniversary of their birth or death. (They also tend to go to temples on the first and fifteenth days of the lunar month, so these are good dates for picture-taking.)

Folk Festivals

Every village has its own folk festival. These are often wonderful events. All along the southern coast and far up the rivers, the annual dragon boat races draw immense crowds. Once religious rites to offer thanks to a woman elevated to goddess status because of her piety and sacrifice for fisherfolk, these delightful races of long, narrow boats with more than a score of hardy paddlers are exciting, shouting gatherings. Visitors are always welcome; join the mobs and scream and clap for whatever team you fancy. It's like Superbowl in every village.

One of the most fun-filled days I ever had in China was in a nameless Guizhou valley where I saw thousands of Dong tribesmen gathered in a big circle. Wandering down to find what was happening, I discovered I had stumbled across a buffalo fight.

This is a gentle procedure. One village brings its bravest and biggest buffalo to face its rival from another hamlet. Much screaming of encouragement and urging of the beasts to battle goes on. Much beer is drunk. Many backs are slapped. Everyone is vastly excited. Even the buffaloes enter into the spirit of things and clash horns, pushing against each other to show which is the stronger beast. Everyone has a great time. The fact that some weird foreign devil has joined the party only makes proceedings that much more lively.

— Chapter Five —

HISTORY

He who reads history
Knows the affairs of the ancients

As one sees a reflection in a polished mirror
So can one know the present by studying ancient times

A few miles downriver from the ancient port of Ningbo in Zhejiang province, the River Yong flows flatly through the paddy fields. A few years ago, some local peasants were digging a pit when they came across some old charred logs and broken pieces of porcelain.

Constant newspaper and radio publicity has made farmers aware of the potential historical value of such finds. They told local cadres what they had discovered. Academics travelled to Ningbo from the provincial capital in Hangzhou to take samples from the ruins near the village of Hemudu. As archaeologists dug, they found not one village but three of them, each built atop an earlier occupied site.

Deep beneath protective layers of silt laid down by prehistoric floods, they finally unearthed a sophisticated log cabin village. Amid the ruins were grains of rice. The significance of their find did not become apparent until the discoveries were carbon-dated in Beijing. The rice cultivators of Hemudu had planted their fields more than 7000 years ago, dating those ancient farmers as the earliest known growers of grain in the world.

Today, those blackened specks of rice grains can be seen in a special museum on the banks of the renowned West Lake in Hangzhou, along with reconstructions of the village of the pre-historic farmers of the Yong River.

Much of China, especially in the north, is sitting atop rich layers of history. Dig down, and you literally are going through the dynasties, as though you are turning a massive book whose pages are metre-thick layers of earth packed with relics of the ages.

One splendid example of this treasury packed in the soil is in Kaifeng in Henan, capital of a dozen emperors. The overflowing Yellow River has over the ages buried this woefully-sited city time and again. The bed of the Huanghe is now elevated six metres above the streets of the town. Every time the river burst its banks in the past, the thick silt settled down over the town. Sometimes, survivors dug out their homes. At others, they simply built a new town on top.

Archaeologists examining the foundations of modern Kaifeng can dig through metres of closely-packed loess earth, finding a new civilisation every few metres. In 1985, workmen laying a new duct for electricity cables and water pipes came across a marble carving. Careful excavation revealed this was part of the magnificent Bridge of Zhou, a famous piece of Song Dynasty architecture that had been lost for 1000 years. Now restored, the carved marble bridge that has featured in many paintings and poems, is a proud historic sight of Kaifeng.

The warrior guards of Xian which have over the past decades attracted hundreds of thousands of foreign tourists were also discovered by accident. Throughout China, mysterious mounds that hide the graves of emperors and the tombs of forgotten kings stand enigmatically amid rice paddies and in northern deserts. Chinese officials have listed so many sites as potential major archaeological treasure houses that it would take centuries for researchers to begin to unearth them.

The Dynasties

The earliest rulers of China were men whose lives are legend. Semi-deities, they are gigantic figures who stride across an enormous historic stage. Like Solomon or Moses in the Judeo-Christian tradition, they are impossibly larger than life, personalities who merge tribal folklore with the actions of individual rulers of early flourishing county-states along the fertile banks of the Yellow River. Nevertheless, there remains a constant but tenuous strand linking the earliest rulers of China with those who followed them onto the Dragon Throne.

The earliest era can be pinpointed to roughly between 2852 BC and 2205 BC. It is known as the Age of the Five Rulers. As with Old Testament rulers, it seems historians of ancient times run the lives of a number of rulers into one reign. The first known ruler, Hao Fuh Hi, is said to have reigned for 115 years, during which he invented writing and stringed musical instruments, organised the clan and family name system and introduced animal husbandry.

The mystical Yellow Emperor, Huang Tai, who is said to have ruled for a century, occupied the throne in 2697 BC. He massed infantry with stabbing swords behind stout shields (like the Roman

Legions 26 centuries later) and conquered widely. He coined bronze money, encouraged medicine, invented boats, reared silkworms and divided his realm into provinces.

His successor, Shao Hao Kin-tieh Shih, ruled for 84 years, according to the old annals, but did nothing more notable than enjoy his reign playing music. Other rulers of the shadowy age, when the Chinese race was emerging along the Yellow River in Shanxi, Shaanxi and Henan, are recorded as reigning for 78 years and 70 years. By the time of the first recorded dynasty, China had reached a level of considerable sophistication that was not to be matched in the western world for another 16 centuries.

Dynastic eras

Xia	– 2100 BC to 1700 BC
Shang	– 1700 BC to 1100 BC
Zhou	– 1100 BC to 221 BC
Western Zhou	– 1100 BC to 771 BC
Eastern Zhou	– 770 BC to 256 BC
Spring and Autumn	– 772 BC to 481 BC
Warring States	– 403 BC to 221 BC
Qin	– 221 BC to 206 BC
Han	– 206 BC to AD 220
The Three Kingdoms	– 220 to 280
Jin	– 265 to 420
Southern and Northern	
Dynasties	– 420 to 581
Sui	– 581 to 618
Tang	– 618 to 907
Five Dynasties	– 907 to 960
Song	– 960 to 1279
Yuan	– 1206 to 1368
Ming	– 1368 to 1644
Qing	– 1644 to 1911

Xia: 2100 BC to 1700 BC

The first cohesive state that rose along the banks of the Huanghe was the Xia. The founder of the dynasty was Yu the Great, remembered and respected still as the ruler who vowed to tame the Huanghe. His promise was kept 4000 years later by the engineers of the Yellow River Conservation Commission who, in tribute to the man who gave them inspiration, raised his statue atop a hill in Henan province. Today, the imposing likeness of Yu the Great stares purposefully across the 16-kilometre wide floodplain confined within massive dikes not far from the provincial capital of Zhengzhou, where he once ruled.

The Xia Dynasty held sway over an increasing area of the rich central length of the river for four centuries, a time when the Chinese race consolidated and combined with other early tribal groups. It was a prosperous agricultural community whose wealth was already based on grain.

Shang: 1700 BC to 1100 BC

Written records of the Shang have been uncovered in surprising quantity. This treasury of ancient literature survived because of the sturdy writing materials used in the era before paper was invented. Some records of the 30 kings of Shang were cast in bronze and describe in considerable detail the daily life and economic structure of the state. Other written remains are inscribed in ideographs on tortoise shells and bones. Shamans would deeply carve their predictions on thick tortoise shells, then put them on hot coals. The shells would eventually split in the heat and from the shards of the shattered written message, the priests would make predictions. Large numbers of these oracle bones have been unearthed. They tell of millet and wheat cultivation, animal husbandry of cattle, pigs, horses, sheep and dogs, of a sophisticated manufacture of silk. Shang bronzes show the artisans of the era were both highly skilled technicians and imaginative artists.

Alas, the era was marred by slavery and superstition. Human sacrifice was common; some graves of Shang nobles have been uncovered and found packed with up to 400 skeletons of subjects killed to accompany rulers to the next world. The Shang domains were extensive, spreading from the Yellow River down to the Yangzi and eastwards to the coast.

Western Zhou: 1100 BC to 771 BC
Eastern Zhou: 770 BC to 256 BC

In the first great recorded revolution, the peasants of the Zhou vassal state in the Wei River valley rose against the Shang. The legendary ruler who founded the Zhou was Qi. His great claim to lasting fame was the introduction of a new type of millet, easier to cultivate and a guarantee of survival for a growing population. He is enshrined as the Lord Cultivator (Hou Ji), the god of agriculture.

Under Zhou rule, China emerged from the shadowy era of myth and legend to accurately dated history. This dates from 841 BC with the publication of the *Table of Twelve Princes*. The Duke of Zhou created scores of principalities under his realm and installed his relatives as local rulers. Constant invasion and incorporation of neighbouring primitive states enlarged the realm. Following in the tradition of their founder, the Zhou rulers improved agricultural techniques over the centuries.

In 770 BC, one of the many tribal leaders, Quan Rong, killed the King of Zhou and established a new Zhou Dynasty.

Spring and Autumn Period: 772 BC to 481 BC

An explosion in technology leapfrogged China out of the bronze age and into the era of iron. Better agricultural equipment could be made with the new material, which was quickly in widespread use. This led to larger crops and a booming economy which in turn encouraged the growth of cities.

Warring States Period: 403 BC to 221 BC

Money was invented, a necessity caused by increasing trade that could no longer be handled by barter. More than 200 mints have been identified from this age.

Qin: 221 BC to 206 BC

The Qin Dynasty did not sit long on the Dragon Throne. But it was under the brutal, intemperate, suspicious and brilliant rule of Qin Shihuang—Great Unifier—that dukedoms, kingdoms, far-flung states and vassal thrones were bonded together in blood and fire into the first true Chinese empire. The emperor was not one to take criticism lightly. If scholars displeased him, he buried them alive. By the hundreds. His legacy to China is vast; a united country.

Han: 206 BC to AD 220

Such was the glory of this era that even today Chinese refer to themselves as Men of Han. The new rulers took the wide boundaries of the Qin and within that vast sweep of territory built an administrative system whose outline can still be seen today. The Emperor Wu, widely known as 'The State', created a vigorous bureaucracy. He was sole authority in legislative, executive and judicial branches with the nation split into small kingdoms and prefectures administered by court favourites and officials appointed by the Dragon Throne. The Han battled wild Huns across the northern borders while at the same time welcoming Buddhist teachings that seeped in from India.

The Three Kingdoms: 220 to 280

Overlapping the end of the Han was a period of chaos during which the northern regions were largely ruled by three competing realms, the Wei, Shu and Wu. A romantic and exciting time, it held long periods of stability and peace for large areas. These vigorous kingdoms were often dominated by assimilated invaders; the Toba tribe which ruled the Wei with intelligence and skill were a Tungusic race from beyond the steppes. Followed by centuries of uncertainty when China was ruled by a confusion of unstable dynasties, the Three Kingdoms are a favoured realm for historical novelists.

Sui: 581 to 618

Rulers of this dynasty were noted for lavishing themselves in extreme luxury. But during this period, engineers planned and dug the Grand Canal which cut from the old homelands on the Huanghe down to the newly rich heartland on the Yangzi. The Sui grabbed local control in one small area of the north, and later reunited competing Chinese clans to eventually gain the Yellow River plain and launch a successful conquest of the southern lands.

Tang: 618 to 907

What the Renaissance was to Europe, the Tang was to China. It was a golden age in which art, painting, sculpture, poetry and other cultural pursuits flowered richly. Not only did the Tang rulers hold onto and expand the empire, they built a cultural edifice whose glory even today reflects on China. Wealthy and peaceful at home, powerful and respected abroad, the Tang forged solid links with surrounding lands and protected the borders by a series of pacts with friendly states. Cities grew into well planned centres of arts, culture and commerce from where mandarins carried out imperial policies.

The era ended in a welter of uprisings and rebellions that resulted in short-lived dynasties. In one of these rebellions, there occurred a harbinger to future anti-foreigner outbreaks; one rebel force sacked Canton and butchered 100,000 Arab traders who had settled there under the benign reign of Tang.

Song: 960 to 1279

Huge areas of China were occupied by northern barbarians when the Song era began. The Tanguts ruled the dusty northwest while in

Manchuria and on the steppes the Khitans held stubborn control. Eventually, a far more formidable enemy was to gallop down and seize the entire northern half of the nation and for most of the dynasty, the Song abandoned the old homelands on the Yellow River and retreated south to establish their capital at Hangzhou. They built it into a city of splendour. Merchants rose in esteem in this period, sponsoring arts and supporting writers, and widespread appreciation grew of the manmade garden. The enemies established in the north were in turn themselves conquered by a new wave of even harsher barbarians, the Jin, who established a dynasty in the north. Soon they were to be swept roughly aside by the most horrific invaders China was ever to suffer.

Yuan: 1206 to 1368

The Mongols came into China with the fury of a fire-belching dragon. Historians estimate they killed 35 million Chinese. They swiftly despatched other barbarian kingdoms, slaughtering everything in their path as they galloped into China, laying to waste huge areas, putting cities to the torch, destroying for the sheer joy of conquest. The Song held on for decades in the south. But their time was limited and eventually the entire realm came under Mongol rule.

Ironically, it was to produce one wise and noble monarch, Kublai Khan, regarded as comparatively mild and benevolent, efficient and incorruptible. This judgement must be tempered by knowledge that he owned all of China and had total control over the lives of everyone in the empire. He expanded the boundaries significantly, winning back all the territory lost by previous dynasties. The Yuan put down rebellions with utmost ferocity and when they shuffled off the centre stage of history, their rule left Chinese territory intact.

Ming: 1368 to 1644

The nation largely rejoiced when a Chinese emperor returned to the Dragon Throne. Nationalism had been making impressive strides during the last years of the Yuan and there was a feeling that all would be well with the world if Chinese ruled China. For a while, that seemed to be the case.

The Ming, putting to use the example of their brutal predecessors, were ruthless. Punishment for misdemeanours was impressively savage; in some cases, the bodies of chastised officials were stuffed and left to hang in their offices to remind new occupants of the post of the need for honesty and efficiency in government. Foreign trade boomed and internally the empire was largely at rest and prospering. Militarily, it was also strong. But it could not stand against a determined, skilful and brave foreign invader.

Qing: 1644 to 1911

The Manchus from the cold plains of the northeast were swiftly assimilated by China. They adapted Chinese dress, cuisine, language and customs and for more than a century ruled the nation with laudable efficiency. A Pax Manchu, similar to the long reign of peace-by-terror instilled by the Pax Mongol, kept the nation quivering in tranquil terror. There was always much internal opposition by Chinese to Manchu rule, today subject of much romanticised novels. It was from this resistance to foreign rule that the triad movement sprouted. For centuries it was a patriotic democratic ideal, only to degenerate into an international criminal conspiracy long after the Manchus finally tottered off the throne at the beginning of this century.

Historic Remains

When it comes to history, China has an awful lot of it. A vast amount has been destroyed. There are two reasons for this. Much of the monumental work—palaces, temples, administrative buildings—were constructed of wood. Over the centuries, it has rotted or burned, leaving little to admire. The tumultuous changes of rule in China saw enormous and widespread destruction. Many emperors,

Upswept eaves of traditional architecture can be seen in every town, but like this one in the Guizhou capital, Guiyang, they are likely to be modern structures.

jealous of the glories of their predecessors, deliberately destroyed the physical evidence of earlier grandeur. Then there were the waves of invaders whose troops saw China as a vast treasury which they could plunder at will. Periods of local uprisings were times of anarchy when chaos reigned and cities burned.

Take the last century or so for an example of how the treasures of China have been laid to waste. The Taiping rebellion destroyed a sizeable section of the south. One of the most wonderful architectural legacies of all time, the Summer Palace of the Qing Emperors, was wilfully smashed and pillaged by British and French troops who saw the act as a punishment for the Chinese emperor breaking an agreed peace treaty imposed after the Second Opium War. Local civil wars and uprisings in Guizhou, Gansu and Xinjiang saw much destruction. The Yellow River broke its banks several times (once when retreating Kuomintang armies deliberately blew up the levees), swamping huge historic areas.

There was the warlord era which saw the nation divided, the Japanese invasion, the civil war; all of these conflicts resulted in much of the past being lost. Above all, there was the organised, state-controlled vandalism of the 1960s when for a decade gangs of hysterical young fanatics roamed the land, encouraged to smash the Four Olds.

They did so with remarkable efficiency, pounding priceless artifacts into rubble, pulling down temples which had stood for centuries, laughing as they smashed relics of the ages.

It is a wonder that so much of China's past has survived.

The Museums

In every city, there are magnificent museums. A trip to museums in any city will be fascinating and show visitors glimpses of the past. Sadly, maintenance in many of them is rudimentary and often there is no non-Chinese printed information available.

The Constitution

It is important to remember that China is in many ways a schizophrenic nation, at once 5000 years old and 40 years young. The intense national pride in the immense and ancient cultural heritage is balanced by constant declarations that the People's Republic was founded only on 1 October 1949, when Mao Zedong stood at Tiananmen Gate and proclaimed: 'The Chinese people have stood up. Now let reactionaries at home and abroad beware.'

This pride in the revolutionary tradition can be seen everywhere. Many buildings and organisations are named with the first two characters Xin Hua, meaning New China.

Guidelines for governing this New China are laid down in the constitution of the People's Republic of China. This is possibly the most inspiring charter ever written. It guarantees freedom of speech, religion, assembly and many other rights.

While the document itself is the very model of an advanced, liberal society, things do not work quite as well in practice. People seeking to exercise many of the rights guaranteed in the constitution are likely to find themselves in a thought correction centre for a couple of decades where they can ponder the error of their ways.

— Chapter Six —

GETTING ABOUT

If a man makes himself friendly wherever he travels,
Where can he go and not find a friend?

Travel in China is hard work. Especially if you are that rare creature who wants to go by himself or with a friend and not as part of a large organised tour group. The transport booking offices are chaotic, confusing and inefficient. The tourist industry staff whose official job is supposed to be to aid tourists are often the least helpful people in the land. Veterans shake their head and proclaim that the only people they met in China who are *not* helpful and friendly are those who are paid to be just that.

But to really get around the country, despite the headaches, nothing can beat going by yourself. It may be frustrating but it can also be a tremendous amount of fun.

In the past, before the age of mass tourism that took off in the late 1970s, foreigners going to China were treated like some rare and delicate form of life. They were herded together like sheep and flocked obediently behind their minders as they shuffled past temples, went into the obligatory kindergarten, snapped their Nikons at the dutiful happy peasants ranged up in a row on a model farm and tramped through a factory where the machinery was clean but obviously unused. The aim was to segregate the cash-paying foreign nuisance from the people and to show them only what officialdom wanted them to see.

How things have changed! In less than a decade, China swiftly opened up most of the nation to foreigners who could travel freely where they wished by themselves. Many who tried this prayed halfway through their odysseys that they had stayed at home and watched a travelogue on television. But once having braved the solitary traveller's road in China and survived, the new Old China Hand could congratulate himself. It was rather like the fellow who stopped hitting himself on the head with a hammer; it was so nice when he stopped. That's how some westerners felt when they departed China.

Money

To the rage, frustration and mortification of many first-time travellers to China, cash is king. Even after a decade of tourism, cashiers in sizeable hotels in large cities are likely to reject traveller's cheques. In most of China, a credit card is an exotic novelty that holds mystical powers; however, you can't buy anything with it.

So you have to carry cash. And lots of it. There are few things that prey on the mind so long as getting back home after a trip to China and recalling that magnificent painting, the wonderful old teapot, the antique prayer rug, the marvellous jar, that you could not buy because you didn't have sufficient cash.

The attitude of what is laughingly known as 'service staff' in old-fashioned Chinese-managed hotels is that you pay cash on the nail. Even if there is a card on display at the counter indicating they take credit cards, they dismiss this with the familiar casual wave of the hand. Why should they go to the trouble of digging out the credit card machine from a dusty drawer and filling in a form? Cash.

Cash

There are two sorts of money in China. First there is Renminbi. This may officially be known as People's Money. But the people don't want it. They want FEC or foreign exchange certificates, which they attempt to prise out of foreigners at every opportunity. In the Alice in Wonderland financial world of communist officialdom, RMB and FEC are valued the same. Nobody else thinks so.

The black market is alive and well in China. Almost everyone dabbles in it because the foreigner armed with FEC or American dollars or Hongkong currency can get twice as much in Renminbi from any street tout as you can get at the official rate in the Bank of China.

What's more, the illegal street currency dealer is a lot more efficient and 20 times faster than the slack, idle, rude and uncaring staff who seem to be unerringly selected to work for the official bank exchanges.

In most Chinese cities where foreign visitors are common, touts linger at the hotel gates. 'Change money?' they enquire. At the Bank of China, it might take you 15 minutes of listening to a girl teller chat to her workmate, read the paper, comb her hair, have a cup of tea before you pass over US$100 and get in return FEC371.27.

Armed with a wad of FEC, you can buy anything. In most antique shops, the inaptly-named Friendship Stores and hotels, you have to use FEC or foreign currency. Taxi drivers like to demand it, too. But in many state-owned stores, you can use the normal currency of China, the Renminbi, to purchase goods such as leather jackets, silks, rugs and other desirable products.

If you go to a state shop with FEC, you pay the same as RMB. For instance, say you want to buy a leather jacket marked RMB280. If you pay in FEC, you pay the same face value in notes, FEC280 or US$75. If you change money with any of the street vendors, you get at least double the official exchange rate. So your well-tailored leather jacket of excellent quality is going to cost you RMB280 which translates into a mere US$45.

Beware. Every so often, the local Public Security Bureau (the coppers on the beat) get carried away with unusual enthusiasm and carry out a crackdown. They grab a few of the touts whose pockets are stuffed with huge wads of FEC, RMB and other currencies. Sometimes, they also collect a handful of tourists in their net. The touts lose their money and go to jail. The tourists are normally chastised and allowed to go.

But if you are a senior executive travelling in China for your firm, or an entrepreneur there to do business, you can be certain the officials with whom you are going to be meeting the next day will know you have been caught dealing on the black market. This can be embarrassing. Any time the authorities want to get nasty—which can happen for unpredictable reasons—you might find yourself suddenly described as a currency speculator. This has happened to American Chinese dissidents, to journalists who raised impertinent issues and to businessmen who have got involved in drunken brawls.

Is it worth the risk? This is something you have to judge for yourself.

Tips

In general, don't bother. Until a decade ago, tipping in China was widely discouraged as a filthy capitalist ploy to bribe the proud proletariat. As with much else in China, times have changed.

Gratuities are still not sought openly in China. But if you receive exemplary service (especially in one of the splendid new western-managed hotels) the staff will not be insulted if you offer them a tip.

As for taxi drivers, guides, doormen and other service staff, tipping is neither expected nor requested.

Beggars are few in China. Those who do approach you are likely to be cheeky children trying their luck on notoriously stupid foreign devils. Smile and wave them away.

Moving Around

There are a plethora of official travel agencies. They have one thing in common. They are universally hopeless.

In any hotel, there is what is called a 'service desk'. This is the communist idea of a joke. 'Service' is a dirty word and the 'service desk' is likely to be staffed by some ill-mannered oaf who is heavily engaged in reading a racy novel. Wait patiently for three seconds, then knock gently on the counter. Apologise for interrupting him at his toil but indicate you want some attention. He will turn back to his book and mumble at you. The women are usually worse than the men.

Patience having failed, you now try another tack.

You go to the manager of the hotel and ask for assistance. 'Ask the service desk,' you will be told. But the service desk is busy reading and cannot give service. 'Sorry, can't help,' the manager will say. 'It is not my department.'

True. The people whose job it is to provide information on city and countryside tours are from the local government travel bureau and the surly youngster at the desk is probably the offspring of some party official who has to be found a berth that pays well and doesn't require too much energy.

If you can find someone to help you, you will discover that every city in China has interesting old environs. You may even strike it lucky and find a brochure outlining these attractions. Armed

89

with a map, you can probably find the way about by yourself.

Local buses cost a few *fen* for long distances and there are always active fleets of private enterprise mini-buses going on main routes. This mode of travel gives you the chance to rub shoulders with the 'broad masses' as the people are referred to in leftist propaganda. It's fun. Once people realise you are not some haughty grandee and are approachable, they are eager to make friends. It's astonishing how often you find someone with a grasp of English, even in the most remote areas.

Escorted tours are best because guides can fill you in on the history of tombs, temples and old buildings. Don't let their absence put you off from exploring on your own, however. It's a lot of fun rambling around old back streets. And it's perfectly safe.

Travel Organisations

China Travel Service fixes visits in China for Overseas Chinese visitors. China International Travel Service does it for foreigners. China Youth Travel Service handles young people on a tight budget. These organisations all have something in common; they are incompetent, largely inept and operate on the basis of doing only what is necessary. However, if you're on a group tour or even travelling by yourself, you've usually got no option but to deal with these woeful bodies.

Usually, staff are totally ignorant of travel arrangements more than five minutes' walk from their office. The people who work there are world champion newspaper readers, telephone users and gossippers. They are not too good when it comes to trying to help visitors.

My tip: The concierge desk at your hotel is probably going to be a lot more helpful in fixing local tours than any tourist agency. Ask them, with a smile, if they can aid you. Plead with them to walk with you over the lobby to discuss possibilities with the 'service desk' of the tourist bureau.

Guides

Dreadful as is the organisation of the big travel departments, and many of the smaller bureaus, too, individual guides are often delightful people. This is especially so if they happen to be that rare Chinese, a person who has a genuine interest in his job.

The system in China is that a young person may be sent to a university to study a language and is then more or less press-ganged into the travel industry. If reluctant to go there in the first place, it's obvious to anyone but a communist bureaucrat that he or she will not put heart and soul into the work. Fortunately for visitors, most guides seem to like their work and to welcome the opportunity it gives them to meet people from abroad and to widen their perspective of the world.

Many guides I have met were charming, humorous, friendly and helpful. They were deeply versed in local history, lore, legend, anthropology, cuisine and a wide variety of other subjects and when questioned about something they didn't know, often went to the trouble to look it up after hours and then phone me at the hotel with the information.

If only the rest of the Chinese tourist industry—and business as a whole—could be as pleasant and efficient as tour guides.

Taxis

It is always a matter of some wonder to me that I end up in cities all over the world directing local cabbies to take me where I want to go. This doesn't only apply in China but happens also in Manila, San Francisco, Sydney, London and in my hometown of Hongkong.

Is there some universal law that states taxi drivers must be totally ignorant of the city in which they drive?

Never get into a taxi in China without making certain the driver knows where you want to go and seems confident he can get you to the destination. Otherwise, you will go for a 20-minute jaunt at the end of which the driver will stop at some pre-ordained spot, turn and smile and indicate that this is where you get off. He takes the money and roars away and after a lot of enjoyable exploration you discover you are in the completely wrong place. Never pay a taxi driver until you have been inside the building and found that he has delivered you to the right address.

Taxis in Guangzhou are excellent. In Beijing, the service is passable. In Shanghai, there are far too few and in many places taxis are exotic novelties. In some places, private enterprise vehicles, the state of which would astound Henry Ford I, are pressed into service. These are normally tiny vehicles of Eastern European origin into which two medium-sized adults can squeeze. Barely. In most cities, prices are fixed in an arbitrary manner. In other words, the cabbies will gouge you for as much as you are sucker enough to pay. Always offer less than half of what they demand. You'll still be paying too generously.

Tourist officials on national and local levels are always telling me that taxis have to use their meters. They obviously do not tell this to the cabbies who flatly refuse to put on their meters. 'Broken,' they say. Then they demand exhorbitant fares. I often refuse to pay and if I think I am being overcharged too outrageously, I call a policeman or one of the special uniformed tourist officials you sometimes find.

'But this will get the driver into trouble,' some people protest. Tough, I respond. If the thief had not tried to rob me unreasonably, I would have happily paid and given a tip. It's not that I mind paying the money, but I do object strenuously to being treated like an idiot.

Have no mercy on unscrupulous taxi drivers. If they try to con you, don't pay them and report them.

Not that the charioteers of modern China seem to fear the authorities. Not long ago in Hangzhou, a cabbie demanded with muttered menaces that I pay FEC10 yuan for a five-minute journey. We explained to him that a few hours earlier we had been talking to the provincial and city tourist bosses who insisted that every taxi in

When in doubt, ask a policeman. He's unlikely to speak English but he will find someone who can. Or, at least, get you to a telephone. I've always found them helpful even though they make it plain you're a pain in the neck.

the famed tourist resort had a meter and the drivers used them.

'I don't care what they say,' the driver snorted. 'They don't scare me. You report me if you like. I couldn't care less. But first you must pay me.'

What's called for here is a bit of the firm smack of revolutionary justice. But in China, taxi drivers seem to be above the law.

Directions

Getting about in China poses problems. Most people don't speak English and attempts by visitors to speak basic Chinese, while appreciated, will probably not be very successful.

So when you venture outside your hotel, always take a hotel card with you that gives the name and address in English and Chinese.

This will ensure that you can find your way back. Ask the hotel's concierge to write your destination in Chinese.

The greatest boon ever to hit China has been the fax machine. If you have an appointment somewhere, telephone the person you are going to see and ask him to fax you directions—written in Chinese and English—to your hotel. Preferably with a hand-drawn map.

When exploring a Chinese city, wander freely. There are no closed areas any more (apart from a few clearly marked military installations where photography is forbidden) and getting about the old core areas of ancient cities is a fascinating experience.

In any sizeable city, street maps are available at hotel book kiosks. They cost a few dollars and are a very worthwhile investment. Make sure before you set out on your first jaunt that your hotel is clearly marked in Chinese on the map. That way, you can point to it and no matter how far you wander, someone will be able to direct you back. Bear in mind that everyone you meet in China will be friendly and eager to help a wayward tourist who has lost his way. But they can't help you if they do not know what you want or where you wish to go. So make sure you always carry the address of the place you are staying and, if possible, a simple map.

Streets

When it comes to naming streets, the present regime has got a lot to answer for. Old names, such as the delightful Bubbling Well Road in Shanghai, are replaced by more utilitarian ones. It is now Nanjing Road.

There is no city in China, as far as I know, which does not have a major artery named Zhongshan Lu and Giefong Lu. Zhongshan is the birthplace of Dr Sun Yat-sen. Giefong means 'Liberation'. Lu, of course, means 'Road'. Anywhere in China, you're pretty safe if you get in a cab and shout Zhongshan Lu. The driver will head to the middle of town because that's where the street is sure to be.

In most big cities, the names of streets are in the *pinyin* version

of Latin spelling. This is a great help in finding your way about with
the aid of a map.

Traffic

The Chinese have a unique relationship with the internal combustion
engine. Vehicles have a propensity to stay in the middle of the road
and to proceed in a forwardly direction at all possible speed. In both
directions. This makes for a great deal of fun for the nervous tourist
quivering in terror in the back seat.

Road accidents are a comparatively new phenomenon in China.
This is simply because until 15 years ago, there was virtually no
vehicular traffic. So how could there be traffic accidents? Since
then, the rare buses, army vehicles and state-owned cars have been
joined by hundreds of thousands of modern trucks, buses and tractors
built in China's own booming auto works and by huge imports of
Japanese vehicles which are used by the tourist industry and for
local transport by joint venture companies. The results are huge
traffic jams in a country with comparatively few vehicles and a
soaring road toll.

Getting a driver's licence in China is an agonising business. For
a Chinese, it requires many months of theoretical study and endless
practical tests including stringent health examinations. So how come,
after such effort, the standard of driving is so appalling?

In the cities, it is not so bad. The newcomer is likely to stare with
a horrified fixed grin of fascination out the window as his taxi
weaves through a sea of cyclists.

It seems the norm that a bicyclist on a Chinese street refuses to
look sideways to see if a car is aimed straight at him over an
intersection. This is apparently on the grounds of what you can't
see, won't hurt you. So pedallers blithely proceed directly across
intersections. Needless to say, they frequently end up under the
wheels of trucks.

At night, the situation is much worse. I have never seen a cycle in China with a light. And outside the centre of every city, the suburbs stretch in a dim, unlit maze of wide, tree-lined streets. Out of the gloom, cyclists appear suddenly. Their vehicles have no reflectors and they are hard to spot. Cars go through city streets dodging cyclists (who seem to be on the road 24 hours a day.) This is made much more fun by the universal Chinese practice of turning off the lights. The reasoning behind this seems to go as follows: Putting on the lights makes the engine tired and uses up more fuel. Therefore, if you don't need to see, turn the lights off. Only turn the lights on when there is a positive need to look where you are going—for example, when a cyclist is about 3 metres in front of you or when the car is going around a dark bend at 80 kph and another vehicle without lights is coming from the other direction. And both are, of course, firmly in the middle of the road.

With an increasing number of foreigners living in China, the former practice of hiring a driver to be on permanent duty is on the wane. People are going to the huge amount of trouble necessary to get a Chinese driving licence. Brave folks. If they are ever involved in an accident, which is highly likely given the customary standard of driving, the foreign devil is *always* going to be held at fault. There will be instant, inflated demands for compensation. People without a scratch will immediately fall victim to agonising, unspecified pains (the Chinese version of crying 'Whiplash!') and getting things straightened out will be a protracted agonising task. I have one friend whose departure from Beijing was forbidden until teams of doctors had made lengthy, week-long investigations of a person who collided with her while both were on bicycles.

My advice to visitors is: Don't even think about driving. If you choose to do so, fully balance the odds. Is it worthwhile to take the risk of going out in a car by yourself or should the independence and freedom of self-travel be weighed against the strong possibility of an accident and the resulting endless bales of red tape this will certainly involve?

Visitors find themselves inevitably trapped in situations where they are captive victims of lunatic drivers. There is no safeguard against this. Up in mountainous Guizhou once, I was in a small bus going over a scenic nightmare of steep ravines and eroded limestone escarpments. The driver seemed to think himself a close relative of racing driver Stirling Moss in a Mao suit; he swung that vehicle around sharp corners, tyres screaming, and roared down unguarded roads with the bus leaning wildly over the side of steep cliffs falling hundreds of metres onto the jagged rocks of wild rivers. The minority folk of the highlands seemed to think this was barrels of fun—more exciting than their cultural gathering of water buffalo fights—and beamed in approval as the vehicle yawned sickeningly on the curves. Not me. I was pale with terror. Coming down into one valley, I spotted a clutch of rooftops. '*Teng, teng!*' (Stop, stop!) I called. The vehicle came to a halt with a screech of brakes and the smell of burnt tyres.

I tottered gratefully out, paid and looked for the local beer stall. Sipping a warm ale in the pale winter sunshine of the mountains, I nodded amiably at the local Dong tribal folk and waited for the next bus. And waited. And waited. Eventually, a couple of hours on, another vehicle hove into view coming down the mountain. Thankfully, I climbed aboard to be greeted by the customary looks of astonishment a foreigner finds in rural China, then by welcome grins as I said hello. I wasn't smiling for long because the bus got off with a start like a fighter bomber taking off from an aircraft carrier and commenced rolling around the frightening corners over the gorges at twice the speed of the bus driven by the former maniac. 'Oh my God,' I said, clutching the seat in front while an aged mountain grandmother beamed at me in approval.

The horrors of road smashes in China are easily witnessed. Most seem to be head-on disasters. Given the popular habit of driving right down the middle of the roads, this is unsurprising. On most stretches of road, pedestrians keep to the side. Then come the cyclists. Then there are small puffing tractors converted to small trucks (taking the part of the water buffalo or draught mule). Swerving past these slowly-travelling road users, heavy trucks swing out to the middle of the road. Passing them on the wrong side of the road are buses and cars. Every vehicle is honking incessantly. So on one narrow lane, you have up to five classes of traveller all going in the same direction at various speeds. Coming in the other direction, the traffic flow is likely to be identical. In the middle of the road, the swiftly-moving cars and buses jostle for position. It is a situation designed for disaster and the end results are frequently seen where two vehicles have slammed into each other head-on. The sights are horrific. So there is ample reason for my fear on the roads; I have witnessed a lot of the end results of this haphazard transport mess.

If the situation is bad in the cities, in the wide open spaces of the country it is far worse, if only because there is comparatively less traffic and the flow is faster. China is supposed to be an atheistic country but any passenger in a car driven by a man in a hurry soon becomes a convert to some belief; you are likely to spend a fair amount of time praying that something is not coming around the blind corner which you are screaming around at 120 kph. It is pointless to ask a driver to slow down or drive less dangerously. He will ignore you. It's his job to drive and drive he shall, just the way he wants to. In past times, it was probably safe to overtake a lumbering truck on a rural road on the crest of a hill or on a sharp blind corner. Chances were, nothing would be coming the other way. These days, with a lot more traffic on the highways, the possibility that another vehicle will be swinging equally wildly around that corner towards you is much more likely.

Roads

Roads in China are generally pretty bad. They differ from province to province. Shandong prides itself on the new series of highways linking its major towns into an economic network. They claim with justification these are the best in the nation. Indeed, the four-lane divided highway system would not be out of place in Europe or America.

In other spots, roads between major centres can be atrocious. The 'highway' between Shanghai and the old cultural city of Suzhou is a case in point. It is a potholed, rundown shambles of a stretch of macadam. In most countries, it would take 40 minutes to cruise down a road between two such great cities. Here, the journey normally takes about two and a half hours with cars, tractors, horse-drawn carts, trucks, buses and cyclists all fighting for their share of the narrow, two-lane track.

Other surprises await in the provinces. In some remote, hilly areas of the southwest, the roads sweeping over mountains and through steep valleys can be excellent.

When you are travelling by road in China, it is not much point asking the driver how far it is to your destination. Rather, enquire how long the journey will take.

Train Travel

When China travels, it does so mostly to the clank of the Iron Rooster. Trains still carry the bulk of the people on their inter-city journeys. For the visitor, a journey by train can be the highlight of a trip to China. In the crowded hard-class compartments, you sit crammed grubby cheek-by-bearded-jowl with the common people. It's one of the best and swiftest ways to meet the normal man and woman from factory and field, the average Chinese people.

Tour guides and government officials will be horrified if any foreigner older than an adventurous back-packing youngster indicates they wish to travel anything but soft- (or first-) class. Indeed, it will be hard for you to persuade a ticket clerk to sell you a hard-class ticket. And I wouldn't advise it for a lengthy journey.

But for a trip of two or three hours—from Shanghai, say, to Ningbo or Suzhou—it can be fun. And it's an adventure. Once aboard, no matter how crammed the carriage, people will squeeze to make a seat for a foreigner. Cigarettes, biscuits and fruit will be offered with a shy grin. Within a couple of minutes, the inevitable English speaker will have come forward and the questions will begin. Where do you come from? Where are you going? What do you think of China? Why is a rich foreigner in the hard class? By the time the train wheezes out of the station and starts clattering along the tracks, you'll be firmly part of the travelling circus that is the Chinese railway system.

With more than 55,000 kilometres of track covering every province and linking the far borders of the nation to Beijing and other great cities, the National Railway Administration is a vital cornerstone of the Chinese economy. It is also one of the most efficient organisations in the land.

This does not mean the visitor can go to a railway station and without difficulty buy a ticket. As with every other aspect of Chinese officialdom, that would be far too easy. Railway service staff are rude, abrupt, incompetent and lazy. As with so many other aspects of 'service', they seem to think the jobs have been provided for them as a rostrum from which they can abuse the public.

Fares for Chinese passengers are kept deliberately low. Foreigners pay three times as much. From Beijing to Tianjin costs US$20 and from Shanghai to Wuxi US$11—far cheaper than by hire car.

If you are buying tickets for yourself, be prepared to stand in line for a minimum of an hour, to face a slothful, slow and idle clerk and then to go through agony before he or she reluctantly produces a ticket. Make sure you have the seat you wish to purchase written out clearly in Chinese, preferably on a railway timetable with the appropriate train marked. Better still, spend the few extra dollars needed and have your hotel or China Travel Service (good luck!) go and purchase the ticket for you.

Realistically, any foreigner travelling as a tourist in China on anything more than a short day trip is well advised to pay to go soft

On a long train journey, book a soft-class seat. This will find you in a four-berth car complete with small table. You can read or doze as the countryside rolls past. Or you can chat with other passengers. On one 34-hour journey from Nanning to Guangzhou, the author shared a cabin with three female electrical engineers going home to Jiangxi province, swapping language lessons.

class. At night, if you are travelling alone, this means you will share a four-berth car with three strangers. It's a good way to make friends. The bedding is warm and clean and as the train rattles through the dark Chinese night, sleep comes easy.

Restaurant cars in most Chinese trains are best avoided, if possible. Most look like mobile pigpens and as you examine tablecloths which appear to have been used to wipe the floor of a public toilet, the thought of hepatitis springs instantly to mind. If possible, have your hotel prepare you a hamper. (My best meal on a Chinese train was across Shandong with fresh German sausage and bread packed by the Huiquan Dynasty Hotel in Qingdao.) But if you are on a lengthy journey, like the three-day Beijing to Guangzhou trip, cross your fingers, point to what looks appetising on other tables and hope for the best. Naturally, there are no English language menus.

One delight for the foreigner on the rails of China is to see the enormous variety of railway engines. The steel tracks are alive with freight and passenger trains and the piercing wail of a steam engine; the chuffing locomotive with its plume of dark smoke is still a common sight. Despite rapid modernisation, steam trains can still be seen, especially if you are away from the major routes.

Toilets

For the newly arrived westerner, going to the toilet in China can be a traumatic experience. Looking back, it can provoke a laugh once safely home. It is seldom so humorous at the time.

The state of Chinese public toilets is normally disgraceful. Even in some large cities, the stand-up urinals for men consist of large upright ceramic jars in which one aims as best one can. The resulting precious liquid is taken away to the nearby fields.

Newcomers are frequently appalled by the standards of hygiene, or lack of any apparent standards, in public toilets. This is partly caused by the Chinese attitude of 'I'm alright, Wong' that reflects a lack of consideration to anyone else. In their homes, Chinese are spotless and so are their toilets. Why should they worry about what sort of mess they leave behind in a public lavatory? How is it their business? They don't intend to go back.

No other single subject fills tourists with such horror. This revulsion is mystifying to many Chinese. What's the problem? they ask as some white-faced American matron stumbles in shocked disarray from a streetside lavatory. Inside, she may have had to use a simple hole in the floor that since its last cleansing had been occupied by a few hundred others.

The saving sanitary grace is the Chinese-style toilet. In modern hotels, railway stations and a few government offices, western style 'sitters' may be found. Elsewhere, the 'squatter' is universal.

For the novice, this may at first be awkward. You have to be reasonably adroit. Practice swiftly makes perfect. A word of caution; remove all money, wallets and other valuables from the trouser pockets before attempting to use a 'squatter' for the first time. Otherwise, you may find yourself attempting to prise your passport or traveller's cheques out of a noisome mess.

'Hey, Harry!'

Years ago, I was at the bustling railway station at Hunghom in Kowloon where the express train to China picks up its eager loads of tourists for the Middle Kingdom.

The splendid station was overwhelmed by a human tidal wave of visitors as soon as it opened. Planned for the days before China opened its doors to the world, when the Bamboo Curtain suddenly swung wide, the new station was instantly packed. The Hongkong authorities had built for large crowds. Besides restaurants, bars, bookshops and banks, there were also adequate toilet facilities.

These offered a choice. Those whose cultural bent was towards 'sitters' could use a western-style loo. For those more used to 'squatters', this variety was available.

Two elderly American retirees wandered into the toilet. Urinals were in the middle. On one side were cubicles of 'squatters', on the other, similar cubicles held 'sitters'.

One of the Americans headed for the Asian-type section where there was a hole in the floor with a flushing mechanism above it. He had obviously never seen anything before remotely like this equipment. He blinked, scratched his head, looked again, then called to his friend.

'Hey, Harry,' he shouted. 'Get a load of this. Somebody's stolen the john.'

Spitting

Health authorities throughout China have engaged for years in public health campaigns aimed at stamping out this highly regarded social custom. They have failed.

Walk down any street in any town in China and you are likely to hear a rumbling, throat-clearing hawking that precedes an explosive expectoration.

Persuasion and education over the past decade has had little obvious impact in reducing the incidence of spitting. So those caught by police and health workers are now given on-the-spot fines. In addition, enthusiastic cadres in the anti-spitting corps are likely to pull out microscopes and require the spittee to go down on his hands and knees to examine what he has just lodged on the pavements.

Beijing Daily and other papers also regularly print the names of those convicted of spitting in public places. But there is little public opprobrium in being known as a spitter so the effect of this move is dubious.

Advice for travellers; try to close your ears but watch your step.

Crowds

In any city in China, there are hundreds of thousands of people standing around doing nothing. Any free entertainment, anything out of the normal mundane flow of life, can produce huge numbers of them at an instant's notice.

Two cyclists collide and exchange angry words; it is street theatre in the raw and the idle flock to listen, take sides, sit in judgement on the rights and wrongs of the incident. A truck hits a bus and it is immediate cause for a gathering that looks like the Superbowl.

A foreigner stopping a policeman to ask for directions with the aid of a map can swiftly become the focal point for a gathering of hundreds. In rural areas where westerners are still rare, the mere

sight of a foreigner sitting down at a streetside stall sipping a beer and eating a bowl of noodles is sufficient to cause children to come running.

The natural curiosity of people and the blankness of their everyday lives combine to create crowds. Let three or four people stop to look at something and soon others gather around. Seeing a clump of people, passersby at a distance drop their hoes or jump on their bicycles and come pedalling to see what others find worth staring at.

Once, in Guizhou province, where I was the first foreigner to penetrate some isolated areas for many years, I went into a toilet in a small town. Five minutes later, I emerged to find myself confronted by a silent crowd of several hundred Dong, Miao and Bouyei tribesmen and Han townfolk who had gathered to look at this weird apparition of a foreigner. '*Ni hao*,' I said, slinging my camerabag over my shoulder. This earned enthusiastic applause.

Such spontaneous rushes of people to look with wonder at the most minor incident can cause apprehension and claustrophobia to the stunned westerner caught in the middle of a human crush. Just say '*Duibuqi*' (Excuse me) and push out of the throng.

105

Fiction

There is probably more nonsense written and believed about China than any other nation. The old, baseless myth about Chinese being inscrutable is one example. Take the Cantonese. Go to a football match and see them shouting, screaming, yelling as they urge on their team. They are about as inscrutable as Sicilians.

Wander through the old brick houses and courtyards that make up the core of most northern cities. If you are a westerner, you will be a curiosity, especially in towns off the tourist beat. People will look at you curiously—why not? You're different. But if you smile, they will flash you a brilliant grin. Say '*Ni hao*' and they will want to chat. Where are you from? Ask at your hotel how to say the name of your country in Chinese. If you are American, learn the name of your state as well.

Soon you'll be surrounded by shy but friendly folk and the chances are some old lady will urge you into her home for a cup of tea. At times like this, language barriers don't mean a thing.

Relax. Enjoy. Smile.

Inscrutable? Don't make me laugh.

Always remember one thing; the Chinese may be proudly different from the rest of the world but, first and foremost, they are people, just like you and I and everyone else. Treat people politely and the chances are they will do the same to you. A smile costs you nothing. It is worth a million yuan.

Good manners are the same in any country. When you are touring in China, you will meet many people. Greet them the way you would back home. Smile, say hello and shake hands.

Never Say No

Chinese people do not like to say NO. They will squirm with embarrassment as they try to find a more diplomatic, tactful and considerate way of expressing the negative. Sometimes, this leads them to great lengths of circumlocution.

This reluctance to say a simple 'No' may seem strange to westerners. But it is part of the Chinese notion of politeness. It is not thought right simply to deny a visitor a request. So instead of just saying 'No' they will go to great lengths to hint that something is not possible, hoping behind the bland smiles that the thick-skinned, hopelessly stupid foreign devil will take the hint.

As an inquisitive reporter with a skin like a Mongolian pack camel, I sometimes find myself pressing officials for an answer about a question.

Over on the Liuzhou Peninsula once, I started to wander away from an organised group visit to an oil refining installation. A few hundred metres away, there were rows of new apartment buildings and I wanted to see what the living standards were like for local people in the 'Houston of China'.

Alarmed, an official came running after me.

Where was I going? To have a look at those buildings, I explained. But, he said, clearly worried, this was not on the programme. It had not been arranged. There was nobody to escort me.

Quite okay, I said. I would just stroll over by myself. Being in the south, people spoke Cantonese, the lingua franca of Hongkong, so I'd be okay. No, he pressed. He gave the standard excuse for explaining the impossible in China. 'It is inconvenient.'

This covers a wide variety of impossibilities from 'It's too much bother' to 'It's punishable by a long jail term.' If you press, as I did, the matter becomes vital. The official became agitated.

Why the hell not? I demanded. I was sick and tired of seeing showplace oil refineries and wanted to see how the people lived.

Out he came with another old chestnut that in China is normally sufficient to end all argument. 'It is not the normal procedure to allow people to go there by themselves,' he explained.

I pressed on over the paddy field dike. He clutched me by the arm. 'Please,' he said. 'It is not permitted.'

It was obvious that if I kept going, he was going to be forced into the position of dreadful embarrassment of telling me bluntly that it was forbidden for me to stray. He was a reasonable fellow and a happy travelling companion so I reluctantly gave in.

As a casual visitor to China, most tourists will probably not encounter the difficulty of forcing someone to say 'No.' But if you make a request to your guide to go somewhere and he seems reluctant, take the gentle hint. Don't put him in a position of having to say 'No.' It will make him lose face and make you unreasonable in not understanding that what you asked was impossible.

Health

Standards of medical care vary widely in China. In the great teaching hospitals in Beijing and Shanghai, they are excellent. So are those in the private, semi-secret hospital in Beijing reserved for the top brass of army, party and government. If you are a normal citizen, however, best of luck if something is wrong with you.

For tourists, the best bet is to hope for the best. No vaccinations are needed for visitors to China but my medical friends advise me to take the shots aimed at preventing hepatitis which is endemic. In 1988, when Shanghai people indulged in their annual gastronomic orgy of eating hairy crabs caught in the lakes upriver, more than a million people came down with this liver disease. Stay away from shellfish, is my advice.

If you break a leg, you will get swift, competent medical care anywhere in China. Anything more complicated is a great deal more problematical.

If you feel seriously ill, contact your embassy in Beijing. They may be able to get you to a reliable doctor. But bear in mind that it is standard practice for all western embassies and foreign companies in China to evacuate sick staffers and their families. At the first sign of trouble, they are on the next Cathay Pacific jet heading down to Hongkong where medical facilities are excellent. I advise you strongly to follow this example.

Hospitals

I must have been to a couple of dozen hospitals in China. All are disgraceful, with the sole exception of the Beijing hospital where senior cadres are treated. I've been there often to see old comrades for whom their personal Long March was coming to an end.

Elsewhere, the situation is grim, grim, grim. In some areas where wealthy Overseas Chinese have funded lavish modern hospitals, stately buildings swiftly seem to deteriorate. In most hospitals, treatment is basic in the extreme. The average local hospital is a drab concrete block with naked steel beds resting on bare cement floors, usually damp.

On one heartbreaking occasion when I was down on the Vietnam border with the People's Liberation Army during one of their clashes with the Hanoi hoodlums, I went to the town hospital where I found a 16-year-old boy paralysed from the neck down. A Vietnamese sniper had taken a potshot at the boy as he worked in the commune fields. Sitting by the teenager's bed was his father, silently clutching his son's hand. Doctors were young men in scruffy white coats. Like their garb, they were unwashed. There were no plans to try to refer the boy to a higher authority or to experts in neck injuries. He was consigned to a living death as a cripple. I wrote to Deng Pufeng (son of Deng Xiaoping) who is a cripple and head of the Chinese association for handicapped people. I offered to fly the boy to Hongkong and for my newspaper to pay all costs for treatment. No answer. It would have been embarrassing for China to admit it had to send someone outside the country for treatment. As far as I know, the boy still lies unblinking and helpless in that noisome, hot concrete box down in Guangxi province.

Emergency, Doctor

Out on the Zhoushan Islands off the coast of Zhejiang province, I was having dinner one night with a gregarious bunch of local winery staff, fisherfolk and officials. It was a merry night for myself and a group of Hongkong-based correspondents and diplomats.

The local wine was sweet red stuff but the first dozen glasses were the worst and after that, along with a couple of cleansing ales and a few toasts of *mao-tai*, the evening progressed well. There was much good fellowship, back-slapping and, at the end of the night, song as people of assorted nationalities stood around the tables and sang national folk songs. All very jolly.

The next morning, however, much of the joviality had worn off and as the bus lurched over hills and around sharp bends, I was feeling distinctly unwell.

'Oh, my God,' I groaned.

What was wrong, one of the local escorts asked.

'I'm never going to drink again,' I vowed. 'I think I'm going to die.'

Never speak literally to a person unfamiliar with a language.

At the next town, we were filing into a hall to hear someone talk about fishery joint ventures with Japan when a doctor, two nurses and a couple of fellows carrying a stretcher suddenly appeared on the scene.

What's up? I wondered.

Then they came over to me, sat me down, took my temperature, blood pressure and pulse.

'Why do you think you are going to die?' the doctor asked, through an interpreter.

It took a bit of explaining until I persuaded him the only medicine I needed was a cold can of Qingdao beer.

Hygiene

Standards of hygiene in China are different from those in the west. The contrast between the gleaming, spick public areas of Japan, the startling cleanliness of Tokyo restaurants and the ingrained filth and dirt of China is striking.

Why? It's hard to explain. Basically, a Chinese looks after

himself and his family. Clean your house thoroughly and sweep the dirt out onto the street. Once there, it's not your concern. Why bother?

Newcomers eating in a local restaurant can be disconcerted by a diner at the next table noisily hawking and spitting on the floor. There's not much you can do about it except pray that his aim is good. In restaurants, if you are nervous about the state of the chopsticks, take a paper napkin and wash the eating implements and your bowl with hot tea.

Water

Better safe than sorry. In every hotel and guest house in China, room staff will bring in a large vacuum flask of boiling water as soon as you check in. Use this. Unless you want to spend a good part of your time in China on the toilet, do not drink tap water.

If your water supply runs out, just take the flask to the desk on the floor of your hotel and give it to the girl or boy on duty. They'll fill it up for you. Chinese don't drink tap water and this is a wise piece of advice to follow.

Xinhua

In every town in China, usually on the main street, there is a Xinhua Foreign Language Bookshop. In bigger cities, these are large and impressive places with an astonishing range of titles in English, German, French, Arabic and many other languages. Most of these books are of such approved 'progressive' authors as Sinclair Lewis, Charles Dickens or John Steinbeck. They are cheap, the quality of printing and binding is excellent and they make impressive presents for young nieces and nephews who need to study good works.

The bookshops also have an incredible array of how-to and technical books. Changsha, capital of Hunan province, is one of the great printing centres on earth and the variety of titles you can see at their annual book fair is truly astonishing.

Xinhua shops (run by the government's international news agency cum propaganda arm) also run to a good selection of maps, posters exhorting you to have one baby and to support the armed forces and to very good inexpensive stationery. Usually close by there is a shop that sells old stamps and in smaller towns where foreigners are not so common, you can snap up some great collector's pieces.

Questions

When it comes to sex and morals, Chinese are surprisingly coy by western standards. The simplest questions like 'Do you have a boyfriend?' will result in furious blushes and protestations. (Official sanctions advise girls to wait until they are 25 to be married, men to hold off tying the knot until they reach 28.)

On the other hand, westerners will be disconcerted by Chinese bluntness on financial matters. How much do you earn? How much did your watch cost? Your camera? Does your wife work? How much does she get? How much does your home cost?

Chinese are quite happy to answer these sort of questions and expect foreigners to do the same.

My advice: Tell the truth. But explain when doing so that although your salary may be enormous when compared with theirs, you have to pay taxes, medical bills, rent or mortgage, school fees and many other expenses which in China are taken care of by the various layers of the state.

Language

It's impossible to learn to speak passable Chinese in a few hours. But you can learn a few simple phrases and the efforts you make to speak Chinese will be greatly appreciated. It will also provide a few laughs, for you and the people you attempt to address. China is a land of many tongues. The Chinese language itself is as diverse as the country. Dialects abound. The Cantonese speaker in the south cannot speak to the Northerner talking in Mandarin.

Here's a culture shock! An American tourist in the port city of Ningbo in Zhejiang spotted a familiar figure on an ice cream machine. Charlie Chaplin is a well-loved man in China.

113

Since 1949, the regime has made great efforts to unify the country by making Putonghua (literally, Ordinary Language) official. It is taught in every school in the land and no matter what language or dialect children speak at home, they learn standard Chinese at school. This is based on the language of Beijing and the north.

The minorities have their own languages which are preserved carefully. But everyone—Tibetan, Mongol, Manchu, Zhuang, Uygur, Yi, Miao, Dong—and all Han Chinese have to go to school in the Ordinary Language. For the first time in history, Chinese from every province can now speak to each other. In the past, and until now in many Overseas Chinese communities, even well-educated professionals had to write in characters to make themselves understood by people speaking another dialect.

On the other hand, Chinese is a very simple language. It stands to reason. After all, tens of millions of children aged three or four years old can babble away in Putonghua or other dialects and if they can do it, surely you can, can't you?

The quick answer (for short-time tourists) is: No, you can't.

The first thing to remember is that Chinese is a tonal language. One sound, pronounced in various tones, can have many different meanings. Take the sound '*Ma*'. It can mean 'mother'. Said with a different inflexion, it can mean 'horse'. Hence the baffling and hysterical stories of foreigners trying to ask someone 'How is your mother?' and, instead, saying to a city dweller who lives in a tiny 6th floor apartment, 'Have you fed your horse?' *Ma* can also mean hemp, numb or to scold. Mandarin has four tones. So a sound like *Gu* (pronounced *Chu*) can tell you 'to go', can mean 'a region', could be exhorting you to 'work hard' or may be referring to a musical score. Take your pick. And good luck.

You think that's difficult? Well, down south in Guangdong, Cantonese has a tongue-twisting *nine* different tones. Think of the embarrassing situations you can easily babble your way into trying to express yourself in that dialect.

Pinyin

There are about 5000 characters used commonly on a daily basis. There are an estimated total of 230,000 written characters and compounds, many of them used in technical, scientific or medical terms; no one person can possibly know them all. But just consider the 5000 common characters. There are only about 400 syllables which the human voice can make to express these 5000 ideas. So the same sound, in different tones, is used. High tone, low tone, rising tone, falling tone ... the way you say a sound determines what it means. A professor at the Beijing Number Two Foreign Language Institute once told me that one sound could be used for 100 various written characters.

In an attempt to try to translate the characters and tones into understandable Latin characters, scholars have for centuries been battling with the baffling tones. There have been many attempts. Most have now been scrapped in favour of the universal Latinisation system known as *pinyin*.

This seeks to translate as nearly and neatly as possible the way Putonghua is spoken into Latin words. It is heavily burdened by legacies of the past when many words and place names were rendered in English under a system used a century and a half ago by well-meaning missionaries. Thus, familiar places like Hongkong became Xiangkang in *pinyin*. Canton turns into Guangzhou. The port of Amoy reverts to its real name of Xiamen.

If you think *pinyin* has no rhyme or reason, explain to an earnest young Chinese student of English why 'koff' is spelt c-o-u-g-h.

Speaking

In Pinyin, the universal welcome is spelled *ni hao*. You pronounce this 'knee how'.

To thank a host for a dinner or a waitress for serving you a drink, you use the common expression for 'thank you', *xie xie ni*. This is pronounced 'shi shi nay'.

Qing is how you say please. Try saying 'ching' to rhyme with 'sing'.

When it's time to go, you bid people *zai jian* or goodbye. The closest you can come to writing this is dzai jee-an. But don't worry. It's a lot easier to say (once you've heard it) than it is to write.

'I'm sorry' or 'excuse me' is *duibuqi*, pronounced 'doi bu chee'.

Pinyin may at first look awkward and difficult to you. It's not easy. But a couple of days of listening to people speak gets you into the rhythm and sound of Chinese patter. The written system may appear clumsy and needlessly complex, but linguists and scholars spent decades perfecting it and it renders spoken Chinese as closely as possible into Latinised script.

Where you from?

The first question a tourist is asked in China is 'Where are you from?' Here are the answers in Putonghua. You're American? Then you come from Meiguo which means Beautiful Country. From England? That's Yingguo because *ying* was the closest Chinese could get to pronouncing the extremely difficult 'England'.

America	Meiguo
Argentina	Agenting
Australia	Audaliya
Brazil	Baxi
Canada	Jianada
Denmark	Danma
England	Yingguo
France	Faguo
Germany	Deguo
Holland	Halan
India	Yindu
Ireland	Aiyilan
Japan	Riben
Malaysia	Malaixiya
New Zealand	Xinxilan
Norway	Nawei
Pakistan	Bajixitan
Scotland	Sugelan
Singapore	Xinjiapo
Wales	Weiyisi

Eating

Eating	*Chi dongxi*
I'm hungry	*Wo ele*
Go to a restaurant	*Qu fanguan*
Food	*Shipin or Shiwu*
Food (Chinese)	*Zhongcan or Zhongcai*
Food (Western)	*Xican or Xicai*
Menu	*Caidan*
Boiled	*Zhu(de)*
Stirfried	*Jian(de) or Chao(de)*
Deepfried	*Zha(de)*
Roast	*Kao(de)*
Steamed	*Zheng(de)*
Hot and spicy	*La*
Sweet	*Tian*
Sour	*Suan*
Salty	*Xian*
Breakfast	*Zaocan or Zaofan*
Lunch	*Wucan or Wufan*
Dinner	*Wancan or Wanfan*
Snack or dessert	*Dianxin*
Chopsticks	*Kuaizi*
Knife	*Daozi*
Fork	*Chazi*
Spoon	*Tangchi*
A bowl	*Yi wan*
Rice	*Fan*
Bun	*Mantao*

Meat	*Rou*	Coffee	*Kafei*
Beef	*Niurou*	Milk	*Niunai*
Pork	*Zhurou*	Mineral water	*Kuangquanshui*
Lamb	*Yangrou*	Fruit juice	*Guozhi*
Chicken	*Ji*	Orange juice	*Juzhi*
Duck	*Yazi*	Spirits	*Liejiu*
Fish	*Yu*	Vodka	*Futejia*
Shrimp	*Xia*	Whisky	*Weishiji*
Crab	*Pangxia*	Brandy	*Bailandi*
Squid	*Youyu*		

Buying

Soup	*Tang*
Vegetables	*Qingcai*
Fruit	*Shuiguo*
The food is delicious	*Hen haochi*

Buying	*Mai dongxi*
I would like that....	*Wo yao neige...*
How much?	*Duosho qian?*
Expensive	*Gui*
Cheap	*Pianyi*
Change	*Lingqian*
Where can I buy...?	*Zai nali keyi mai...?*

Drinking

Drinking	*He dongxi*
I'm thirsty	*Wo kele*
Let's go to the bar	*Qu jiuba*
I want to order...	*Wo xiangdian...*
Beer	*Pijiu*
Ice water	*Bingshui*
White wine	*Baijiu*
Red wine	*Hongjiu*
Bottoms up	*Ganbei*
Tea	*Cha*

Walking

Left	*Zuo*
Right	*You*
Forward	*Wangqian*
Stop	*Ting*
Up	*Wangshang*
Down	*Wangxia*

Writing

Some bemused visitor once remarked that Chinese writing looked like what snails left behind after they crawled over a flagstone. Anyone with a simple grasp of the language sees the convoluted characters as things of beauty.

Basically, the system of ideographs was based on pictures. Every idea had a picture that expressed it. Gradually, the pictures became more stylised and simplified, a process that continues today as Chinese scholars strive to make common characters easier to read and write.

Take the symbol for sunrise. It was once a complex picture of a sun with beaming rays rising over the horizon. Now, it is shown as a box with a line through the middle. It is also, incidentally, the first character for the name of Japan, Land of the Rising Sun.

The first character for China, is similarly simple. It is a box with a line through the middle, but up and down instead of side to side. This character means 'central', and is the first character of Zhong Guo or Middle Kingdom.

The commonly seen character *shan* or mountain began as a picture of a range of mountains and developed over thousands of years to the simple sign used today. Many other characters have also changed in this fashion.

When it comes to new characters for new ideas, especially in technology, the awkwardness of written Chinese becomes obvious and only experts can recognise many of the very complicated characters used in science, computers, medicine and research, which are completely unknown and virtually indecipherable to most laymen.

A tip for tourists: Buy yourself a simple book on written Chinese and try to learn two characters a day. You'll be surprised at how soon you pick up some of the basic ideograms and the history of how the written language has developed is a gripping intellectual jigsaw puzzle that can provide much enjoyment.

A Good Laugh

The Chinese people have a sense of humour that can sometimes be baffling to westerners. They laugh uproariously, slapping their thighs with deep appreciation of things which would leave Europeans either unmoved, mystified or appalled. The sight of someone falling down a flight of stairs can provoke outright laughter. Often, this mirth covers embarrassment.

Chapter Seven

DOING BUSINESS

Amiability begets riches.

The Three Ps

There is no great secret about doing business in China. Just follow
the tried-and-true lessons of the Three Ps. This is a remedy that has
been handed down by veterans of the China trade. It preaches that
to do successful business in China you need large reservoirs of three
personal attributes.

The first is patience.
The second is patience.
The third is patience.

After you have exhausted all the above, when your teeth are gnashing, your blood pressure is soaring and your ulcers are acting up, then reach deep into your mental reserves and ... be patient.

'Have a Rest'

You catch an aircraft in Hongkong for the 20-minute hop up the Pearl River Delta to the old trading port of Guangzhou. Immigration and customs are swift and pleasant. You stroll out of the terminal and, if it is your first trip and you have business appointments, you are met by a young official who speaks your language. He is probably from the Foreign Affairs Office of the factory or government office with which you plan to hold negotiations. He or she will be polite, friendly, knowledgeable and have your best interests at heart. There will be a car waiting and, if not, the interpreter will go with you in a taxi to your hotel.

Once checked in, your new friend will shake you by the hand and bid you farewell.

Wait a minute! What's happening? Who am I going to see? Where's the factory?

Oh, no, it will be explained. Not yet. Not possible. You have come all the way from Hongkong. You must be exhausted. Have a rest.

But, you protest, you don't want to rest. You want to work.

You will be greeted by a patient smile. Work later. Rest first. Do not worry, everything is arranged. This afternoon, after you have rested and had a good lunch, then you can go to the factory where the 'responsible officials' will be waiting to receive you.

But first, have a rest.

Welcome to China. That's the first half day wasted.

Footing the Bill

It is an indisputable fact of life that every single foreigner, particularly westerners, is a multi-millionaire. If they are not personally rolling in hard currency, then their companies have unlimited wealth and the visitor to China has a personal spending budget and expense account that allows him endless luxury. This rosy picture of life in the west is an accepted fact in China.

Therefore, arrangements are made—without consultation—in accordance with this perception of the capitalistic wealth of the foreigner. If you have made arrangements to see the Ministry of Light Industry in a provincial capital, representatives of the Foreign Affairs Bureau of the department will be at the airport to meet you. Hands will be shaken, greetings extended, cards exchanged and the new arrival will be ushered into a luxury car (probably Japanese) for the trip to the city centre where arrangements have been made to lodge you in the finest (foreign joint venture) hotel.

All well and good. What you have not been told, and what you will never be informed of until the day you depart and are handed a hefty bill, is that you are being charged for every last cent. The car is on your bill, sometimes costing FEC120 a day. It may sit in the shade with the driver snoozing all day long. Even if he never puts the key in the ignition, it's going to cost FEC120 a day. Into your hotel will move the provincial bureaucrats assigned to 'assist' you. They have made themselves comfortable in a suite for which you will be charged and even if you seldom see them, they will devour three or more hearty meals a day for which you will probably pay.

Irate businessmen claim with rage that they often think they are being treated like honoured guests only to find when it is time to book out that they have been mistaken for a Rockefeller come to dispense largess. Grasping, gouging tactics aimed at squeezing every last cent out of the visiting businessman are now discouraged. The message that westerners are not all rich and cannot all afford to support huge teams of hangers-on while trying to fix a workable deal is slowly penetrating Chinese bureaucracy.

But to be on the safe side, always IMMEDIATELY on arrival ask what you are paying for. Is the car on your bill? If you don't want it, say so. Who is your escort officer? Are you being charged for his time by his department? How much? What exactly are his duties? If you are doing business in a city centre and do not want a car, say so. Taxis in many cities are now reliable and cheap. But always find out—preferably before you go to China—precisely what it will cost you.

Be prepared to spend for a banquet and for a similar level of entertainment of contacts as you would in any other country. But do not let yourself be taken for a sucker. There are still many smaller cities in China where the advent of a foreign businessman is looked at as something akin to Santa Claus arriving with a well-laden sleigh.

Oriental Mañana

To the go-go western executive and entrepreneur who wants to get things done quickly, working in China can be a frustrating experience. The motto is similar to the old army adage: Hurry up and wait.

Until 1986, the after-lunch snooze was a standard feature of Chinese business life. Most offices had cots on which civil servants could sprawl for two or three hours to regain their strength after an exhaustive morning of reading *People's Daily*, drinking tea and making a few phone calls.

The deep sleep lasted at least two hours and could easily, in the sultry summer months when the deep, humid heat settled on the cities, extend generously past this. Rousing reluctantly from this badly needed siesta, the cadre would stretch, go to the toilet, have some more tea and ponder the possibilities of dinner.

This sedate pace of life was shattered rudely in 1986 when that bustling octogenarian Deng Xiaoping declared the afternoon siesta outmoded in the era of faxes, satellites and China rushing towards modernisation. There was much muttering among the paper shufflers of the vastly over-staffed bureaucracy. No sleep in the afternoon? Impossible!

Even today, a deep and impenetrable hush settles over many a government office from noon until mid-afternoon. First it's a hurried lunch in canteen or noodle stall. Then it's back to work for a sleep.

Things are not as bad as a few years ago when a post-prandial snooze was almost compulsory. But if you should arrive for a mid-afternoon appointment and find the cadre you are supposed to meet rubbing sleep out of his eyes, don't be surprised.

The Work Ethic
One of the great mysteries of the east is why Chinese societies outside China are invariably so vastly efficient, successful and profitable while inside the People's Republic, the giant slumbers slothfully on.

There are many theories.

Look at Singapore where Overseas Chinese have helped to create a gleaming financial city-state. Observe Taiwan, penniless in 1949, where the standard of living now rushes towards that of Japan. Cast a fearful eye at Hongkong where six million workaholic Cantonese have made toil and conspicuous consumption the popular state religion. Chinese dominate the commercial life of Thailand,

125

the Philippines, Malaysia and Indonesia. They are heading the same way in California, Australia and British Columbia.

So what's wrong with the Chinese who stay home? Nothing. It's the system. The past four decades have crushed the initiative and enterprise out of the entrepreneurial nation. Under communism, if you were wise, you kept your head down and were as inconspicuous as possible among the other billion fellow citizens of the New China. You didn't make waves. And you certainly didn't try to make money.

With the new reforms of 1978, things changed suddenly. The shackles of outmoded Maoist theory were broken. People could work for themselves.

The Chinese urban middle class reacted hesitantly at first. They had heard many glowing promises in the past of economic reform, only to have them nipped swiftly in the bud. But this time, things were different. Comrade Deng meant what he said. Slowly at first, then with swiftly gathering impetus, the Chinese people hurled themselves into business.

The Iron Ricebowl

Enshrined in modern Chinese life as deeply as a state religion is the concept of the iron ricebowl. Put simply, this means a commitment by the state to provide a job for life. The pay is not good, the position may be humble, the task may be boring ... but come hell or high water the system means that you've got a guaranteed job until the Yangzi runs dry. Trouble is, as a generation of frustrated foreign businessmen have ruefully discovered, the system simply does not work. It has in-built faults that invariably result in lost production, delays, breakdown of equipment due to lack of routine maintenance and factories missing deadlines for orders.

For anyone who has been in a factory or workplace in the west, going into a Chinese state-run enterprise is a vastly illuminating experience. The problems of China's appalling productivity rate can be easily seen. Most factories are grossly overmanned with a half-dozen slackers assigned to a job which could be handled easily by one efficient worker.

In a steel factory in Guangdong a few years ago, I was being

127

shown around by some senior cadres. We walked through the foundry and scores of 'workers' were loafing around the plant. Those who were not sitting around reading newspapers, sipping tea or chatting with friends had spread newspapers on benches or floors and were sleeping the just slumber of the exhausted. After all, they had turned up to work, hadn't they? What more was expected of them? Not a great deal. In another society, such on-the-job laziness would have meant dismissal. Not in revolutionary China. The workers took no notice at all of the cadres, who in America or Europe would have been the equivalent of members of the board and chief executive officers of the company. They knew they could not be sacked.

Breaking the Ricebowl

Seeking greater efficiency, trying to boost the wealth of the country, the new policies introduced in 1978 called for a revitalisation of industry. The old slack habits of the Maoist past could not be tolerated in modern plants, especially when foreign investors were asked to pour in millions of dollars.

As new management techniques—a fair day's work for a fair day's pay—were introduced, the most dishonest, idle and lazy of workers were sacked. This came as an enormous shock to a workforce which for 30 years had come to think of going to work as an opportunity to relax.

The iron ricebowl system had inherent faults. Why should Comrade Wong work arduously and conscientiously if Comrade Chan spent the day reading the *People's Daily* and Comrade Li played cards and Comrade Tsai crawled into a corner and dozed? All got exactly the same pay and privileges. Each of them had a tiny apartment that was virtually rent free, enjoyed the same subsidised food and got the same miserable pay. So why should one person work while a dozen did as little as possible?

All this ended when the responsibility system was introduced. Then diligent Wong got promoted and earned more pay, Chan got paid on piece work only for what he produced and Li was criticised by other members of the workforce because his slackness was affecting overall productivity and eroding the value of bonuses paid for production. Comrade Tsai was warned to work or be sacked. The results were astonishing. In factories where workers were paid on piece rates or where staff enjoyed profit-sharing bonuses, production immediately soared.

Quality

In its headlong rush towards industrialisation, Chinese industry has made many basic mistakes. These are admitted by central government planners who frankly confess the country was overwhelmed by the pace of development.

The basis of many complaints by foreigners doing business in China is the lack of quality control. They complain that the attitude 'near enough is good enough' is widespread throughout the country. But goods produced using this work philosophy are certainly not good enough for most end-users.

Examples abound. A hopeful American who signed a multi-million dollar contract for rubber surgical gloves went broke because the material had microscopic holes that would allow the deadly AIDS virus to penetrate the gloves. Therefore, his western customers refused to accept them.

When an American automotive company established a joint venture with China to produce the Beijing Jeep, every single part produced by local plants had a fault.

The American on-site manager complained. To no avail. Then he took the unprecedented step of writing a personal letter of complaint to the then party boss, Zhao Ziyang. He explained the situation, described in detail how his Chinese joint venture partners had broken promise after promise and said that if things were not made good promptly, he was going to pack up and American Motors would simply cut their losses and pull out of China. Forever. Results

129

came as swift as a summer lightning blast. One of the nation's top economists (a can-do bustler named Zhu Rongji, now Mayor of Shanghai) was sent to sort things out. The money owed to the Americans flowed in, the plant was saved.

The moral of this story is simple; if you are in a deal and it is going sour, do not grimly hold on and keep losing money. State your cases plainly to the most senior official. Then, go to the press, both local papers and international publications that circulate in China. Call press conferences in the city where your factory is sited, and in Beijing and Hongkong. If the worst comes, cut your losses and pull out. In the post-1989 climate, with China desperate to attract and retain foreign investment, tough talking works wonders.

Do not allow yourself to be strung along by lying, incompetent and dishonest cadres. Be firm. Stand fast. Insist they meet their end of the agreements. And if they don't, scream loudly to the press.

Disputes

In a large industrial undertaking anywhere, there are likely to be disagreements between partners. In a country long addicted to strict Marxist theories, short of foreign currency and believing that the world owes it a living, this is particularly so. When the foreign partner is a hard-headed, tough, shrewd capitalist who refuses to bow to blackmail and threats, such disputes are likely to be spectacular. Take the case mentioned above of Don St. Pierre and Beijing Jeeps.

Because of shoddy workmanship of parts and lacklustre management, not to mention labour idleness—this promising licensing venture came perilously close to disaster in 1986. The Chinese had no money during one of their periodic economic slow-downs. They refused to pay for the American kits needed to assemble the vehicles.

Infuriated by constant delays and arguments, the forthright American had a personal letter delivered to then Premier Zhao

Ziyang. If the cash was not forthcoming, the Yanks would go home, he said. As well as taking the dispute to the top ranks of the Chinese leadership, he also took it to the press. Hurriedly, a senior negotiator stepped in and after a week of tough negotiations the Chinese paid up. The project was saved and is now a success.

The result of the face-to-face confrontation was surprising. Suddenly American Motors began to get full cooperation.

The lesson is obvious, say veterans of China's growing business scene. Foreigners should be as cooperative as possible but when a situation gets to crisis point, it should be made absolutely plain that things are so unsatisfactory that it is time to pack bags and head home—and that the situation will hit the headlines in the international press.

A Billion Consumers

When ping-pong diplomacy swept aside the Bamboo Curtain in the early 1970s, international businessmen poised ready to swoop on what they saw as the greatest commercial prize in history. In front of them, hungry for western consumer goods, were a billion potential buyers. They saw a bonanza.

Trouble was, as many multinational executives and ambitious entrepreneurs were soon to discover, that enormous marketplace was populated by paupers. The five million striving capitalists in Hongkong had more money to spend than the vastly numerous compatriots over the Shenzhen River.

Many of those who dived so eagerly into the frothy waters of the newly opened Chinese market emerged sodden and sad.

In the treaty port era, the slogan that guided businessmen was 'oil for the lamps of China'. If the western oil companies could corner the market and provide the kerosene to provide light in millions of Chinese homes, it would add up to big profits. The same sort of philosophy guides many modern-day businessmen. If every Chinese could just be persuaded to buy a Japanese bedside clock or a pair of Italian shoes or a pair of American jeans, all would be well with the world. They forgot that the Chinese peasant had scant few yuans with which to purchase such consumer goods. And the Chinese government was not keen to see people fritter away currency on such fripperies. No, what Beijing wanted was the west to invest in modern plants that could use Chinese materials to make goods that could then be sold to the outside world, bringing hard currency into the national coffers.

There was a fundamental difference in perspective.

A Different Market

A few years ago, standing in the Corner Bar of the China Hotel just across Liu Hua Road from the Trade Fair building in Guangzhou, I fell into conversation with two American traders.

Both men had gone to China's biggest fair to sell, not buy. What they were selling and the success they had illustrates how China is a very different market to the rest of the world.

One man was selling used bus and truck tyres. Under American regulations, these had served their safe life's work and were destined for the scrap heap. By Chinese standards, the tyres had tens of thousands of miles of use left on their treads. He sold the lot to enthusiastic officials from many provinces and got agreements stretching far into the future to sell a lot more.

He was jubilant.

The other man was not so merry. He had journeyed all the way to China to sell cheap but reliable and efficient electronic gadgets. You attached one of these to your garage door and put another in your car. When you drove home, the garage door automatically opened so you could drive straight inside.

Terrific! Except that in 1983 there was not one single private car in China and nobody had a garage.

He didn't make a single sale.

Exchanging Cards

If you are in China as anything except the most casual of tourists, you *must* carry business cards. And plenty of them. Even if you are travelling as a simple sightseer, the possession of a bundle of cards saying who you are, what you do and where you come from will come in very handy and smooth your passage. If you are there on business, cards are absolutely essential. Without your *ming pian* (business cards) you scarcely exist. If you don't have them, you certainly are not a person of any importance.

Cards should be simple. If your company or association has a logo, this likeness should be carried on the card. Then there should be your name, title and position, a mailing address and a telephone.

The card should tell what sort of work you do. For instance, if you are sales manager of a company named John Brown and Sons, the card should indicate if the company makes wine, builds ships or buries people. On the reverse side, the same information should be in Chinese. Remember that a lot of the people you meet may not be able to read or speak English. Most sizeable towns in the western world can now arrange to have bilingual cards printed. If not, you can have them done swiftly in Hongkong, Singapore or any other Asian city heading towards China. If you go direct to China and find yourself without proper cards, your hotel can probably have some quickly whipped up for you. The cost will be worthwhile; proper cards will oil your introduction and help you in your initial steps to doing successful business in China.

When introduced, shake hands, say '*Ni hao*' and then hand over your card. The card should be passed over, held in both hands. You should also use both hands to accept cards offered to you; that's the polite way.

Making Acquaintance

Basically, introductions should be made in China in the same way as in the west. Introduce most senior members first. If your company has a delegation, the highest-ranking member on your side should be introduced to the senior representative of the Chinese side.

In an informal setting, the oldest people present should be introduced first, reflecting the traditional Chinese respect for age. All else being equal, a woman should be introduced to a man. 'Miss Wong, I would like you to meet Mr Smith.'

As anywhere on earth, younger people are likely to be far less formal than their elders. But to be on the safe side, when introduced to a Chinese of any age, shake hands, smile and say 'Hello' in Chinese or your own language.

Taboos

Chinese men often hold hands with other men. There's nothing sexual in this, merely a show of friendship. Western men in China are sometimes embarrassed when a Chinese to whom they have just been introduced casually pats their thigh or drapes an arm over the shoulder. It's not meant to be offensive, merely a relaxed demonstration that you've been accepted as a pal.

Much greater care has to be taken between the sexes. The western practice of kissing a newly introduced person of the other sex on the cheek is shocking to Chinese mores. Never do it. Shake hands instead in welcome or farewell.

Names

Names are serious things to Chinese, especially the family name. It's polite to remember them. Mr Wong will be distressed if you call him Mr Lee.

The Chinese way with names is simple and logical. The family name is given first. Hence, Mao Zedong is Mr Mao. In the case of the late chairman, Zedong, the given name, means Very Clear East. The given name is the equivalent of the western Christian or first name. Thus Chan Mei-ling is Ms Chan. (Mei-ling means Beautiful Intelligence.)

Unlike Chinese communities in the west and in places like Sarawak or Hongkong, very few Chinese in the Mainland have adopted western names. Those who have probably work in a western-run hotel or some other organisation connected with tourism.

In such cases, you might come across a person with a name like Irene Wong Chan Mei-ling. This can cause confusion to a newcomer to China who wonders what on earth he is supposed to call her.

Here's the explanation; Chan Mei-ling is married to Mr Wong. She also has adopted a western name, Irene. So she is Mrs Irene Wong. Or Ms Chan. Or Mei-ling. Or Irene.

So what do you call her if you want to be polite? Either Madam Wong or Miss Chan.

And you will normally call business contacts by their surname even if you have known them for a long time. If you stick to calling Vice-Director Li, Mr Li, you can't go wrong. Trying to use his given name, Kwok-wen, for instance, can lead to needless misunderstandings.

Keep it simple.

Communication

Facsimile machines are ubiquitous in China. The reasons are simple. While it is extremely awkward and time-consuming to transmit a message in Chinese characters by telex, it is easy as pie to do so by fax. To send a telex, every ideogram in a message has to be looked up in a translation book and the appropriate number noted down. Then the message, in the form of a long string of numbers, is telexed. At the other end, the message is studied by a postal authority staff member who consults a book that lists numbers and characters. The message is then written out in Chinese characters. If you want it in English, it has to be translated.

Given the slackness and lack of any sense of emergency by most Chinese junior bureaucrats this is a system that could have been custom-designed to ensure frustration and rage. Hence the joy and delight with which the facsimile revolution has been welcomed by Chinese and foreigners alike.

The Chinese mail system is excellent. Why? This is yet another of the Great Mysteries of the Orient. Most Chinese public services are a disgraceful joke but the posts are swift, efficient and certain.

Telephones are another matter. The IDD system that now links most modern hotels to the outside world is superb. The interior telephone system is ramshackle, unreliable and tends to operate at the whim of telephonists on hotel switchboards and city exchanges.

Telephone manners take a bit of getting used to. Say you call a factory and want to be put through to the manager. The telephonist demands to know who you are and what you want. Then you get put through to some other nameless functionary. A similar telephonic interrogation is held. Finally, you get the great man's secretary. Where do you come from? What is your name? What is your company? Why do you want to speak to Mr Wong? Does he know you? Is he expecting your call? After a grilling that makes the Grand Inquisition seem like mild, child-like whimsy, Mr Wong eventually comes on the line. He is debonair, helpful, pleasant. When you get to know Mr Wong over a banquet and a couple of glasses of *maotai*, you query him about the barriers. Why is it so difficult to get him on the phone? He professes astonishment. No such instructions have been given. Is it nosiness by impertinent staff? Is it overzealous secretaries trying to protect the boss from unwanted callers? Is it sheer stupidity? I suspect a combination of all three, plus a healthy dollop of snooping by underlings.

And remember, any telephone number in China is treated as a state secret.

The Reception Office

They are identical all over China. The bleak layout is the same, the furniture looks as if it was mass produced for the purpose in a factory that has not changed design since the 1940s, and after a dozen meetings in reception offices all over China, the visitor begins to swear the same tea is being poured from the same pot by an infinite variety of twin sisters.

Be it government office or manufacturing plant, the welcome for the foreigner is warm and genuine. The Reception Officer (surely, he must have some other duties in addition to welcoming guests?) shakes hands, exchanges cards and escorts you to the Reception Room. Almost invariably, this is up a flight of concrete stairs to the third or fourth floors. If there are lifts, chances are the electricity is turned off or the operator is out for lunch. Up you trudge.

Once inside, there is a familiar scene. Around all four walls are arranged low-slung, soft sofas. In front of these, arranged with the precision of a People's Army parade in the Square of Heavenly Peace on National Day, are equally low tables. The sofas are usually covered in uniform green material. The tables have glass tops with embroidered doilies underneath. The cups are traditionally handless with matching covers to keep the tea warm.

You sit. The cup is filled. You wait. Sooner rather than later, the official you have come to see arrives. You are introduced by the

137

Reception Officer, you go through the etiquette of exchanging cards. The VIP sits on the couch, usually directly opposite the door. The visitor sits next to him, on the right. The interpreter gives a welcome speech.

The Brief Introduction

Then comes the infuriating waste of time of The Brief Introduction. This can be a lengthy ramble through history, geography, climate, agriculture, habits and other facts, figures and fantasies. The visitor is often treated as if he is an illiterate and the very basic facts of life have to be patiently explained—yet another example of how Chinese treat backward outsiders. If you have done your homework, the endless litany of The Brief Introduction can be agonisingly boring.

Most people who travel to a specific destination in China, especially for business, have done their ground research. Local officials, especially in provinces off the commonly beaten track, take no chances. In 1989, the two authors went to Taiyuan, capital of Shanxi province in the north, to research and write a series of articles on coal, power, minerals and industry in this resource-rich area which is also one of the cradles of Chinese civilisation. We had more than a dozen meetings. The start to each was similar. In would come an official. Hands would be shaken, cards exchanged, welcomes extended. Then would come The Brief Introduction.

Every official—at three or four meetings a day!—would commence by pulling out a handwritten brief obviously copied laboriously from a textbook. He would then proceed to ponderously read. Shanxi, he would announce with great satisfaction, had an area of 156,266 square kilometres and a population of 24.76 million people. The capital, Taiyuan, was at an altitude of 800 metres above sea level and was in the exact centre of the province, which occupied the high loess plateau. On they droned. And on. And on. And interminably on. There was no stopping them. First time, it was bad enough. By the 12th performance, both of us could almost chant along in Putonghua, with a strong Shanxi accent, the statistical account of the province, its peoples and its industries. Only after each official had got to the end of his own personal version of The Brief Introduction, could we begin asking questions.

It is a tactic familiar all over China. Local officials want to introduce their area, be it a small town, a city, a regional district or a province. They are trying to be helpful. They have gone to some trouble to gather the facts and figures. It is no use taking the Reception Officer aside and hinting discreetly that you have heard it all before; you are about to hear it all again. The chances are, you have amassed all these details as routine background before you left home. No matter. The Brief Introduction rolls on as certainly and as inexorably as the Yellow River rolls down to the sea.

Grin, sip your tea, nod periodically and pray for it to come to an end.

Interior Pollution

Cigarette addicts are unrepentantly puffing away in China. The health fad that has had nicotine fiends stubbing out the evil weed in other parts of the world has not affected China. The result is decided discomfort for those who don't like sitting in a smoke-filled room.

On one trip to a Chinese provincial capital, I went to a briefing by top officials. When I arrived on time at 2.30 p.m., the 15 men who awaited me had evidently been in the reception room for some time; I walked through the door and the smog had me groping for my seat.

All 15 men were chain smokers. They would light up cigarettes made from the powerful local tobacco and happily puff away. As soon as they finished one coffin stick, they put it aside to smoulder in the ashtray and lit another.

The room was choked in smoke. The windows were tightly sealed to keep out the winter chill. My eyes streamed. I coughed constantly. The fumes continued.

It is no use whatsoever asking Chinese not to smoke. You will be considered very rude if you do so. The only solution is to try not to breathe, to cut the interviews as short as politely possible and to stumble out for a lungful of clean air.

Who's in Charge Here?

This is a good question. Sometimes, nobody seems certain. Partly this is because of the jobs-for-the-boys syndrome so richly beloved and deeply entrenched in Chinese life. At other times, it is because of the confused power structure in which a corporation manager may have equal status with the factory's party secretary. Sometimes one of them answers a question, sometimes another.

If you are a businessman seeking a session with the top man who can make a vital decision, you are likely to spend a couple of days speaking to officials of various levels. Your first contact will be with the local government or corporation's foreign affairs office. Then you will meet the economic and export officials in charge of exports.

Finally, you will meet a person whose title on his business card will probably announce him to be the Deputy Director or Assistant President. Don't be fooled by this. It is similar to the Vice-Chancellor of a British university. The Chancellor is a respected figurehead; its the Vice who's got the clout.

Same in China. The deputy or assistant is probably the top decision-maker. The man who enjoys the prestige in the top slot could be some aged veteran of the Long March who has never been to the factory or office, apart from turning up to head the table at welcoming banquets.

I recall once down in the Liuzhou Peninsula in southern Guangdong toasting the President of a 2500-room luxury hotel for foreign oil workers. We were at the same table eating a 16-course banquet of local specialities. How long had he worked at the new hotel in Zhangjiang? Eight months, he said. Where had he worked

Business in China is sealed with a drink as well as a handshake. Be prepared to soak back firewater like this fiery liquor being offered by a Beijing waitress.

before? For the government. What part of the government, I persisted? In the army? Doing what? I rudely kept on. It turned out, he was a venerable old general who had been given the hotel job as a communist equivalent of a golden handshake, a plush retirement benefit near his home county. The hotel was being run on a day-to-day basis by a 29-year-old Hongkonger.

The Eleven Commandments

Negotiating a deal in China can be an agonising procedure. The Chinese have been doing business for a long time and are often prepared to talk for weeks, months—sometimes years!—before signing an agreement. Time is on their side and they will hold out for the best deal they can get.

To cope with the endless, frustrating sessions of negotiations, visiting entrepreneurs have to prepare. Veterans have drawn up a list of suggested rules to follow:

1. Patience
2. Perseverance
3. Stamina and persistence
4. Friendly sincerity
5. Firmness to press your point
6. Flexibility
7. Tact and a sense of humour
8. Technical knowledge of the product
9. Simple clear language to ensure accurate communication
10. Honesty and frankness
11. Ability to sit through endless banquets, drink gallons of tea and toast your potential business partners with such potions as snake wine, *fen* (herb) bamboo spirit and the dreaded *mao-tai*.

Mutual Benefits

Traditional Chinese business philosophy holds that all parties involved in a commercial agreement should be happy and should make a profit. In the best of all possible worlds, this would be a laudable aim. In reality, it doesn't always work like that.

When China first opened its doors a decade ago, there was wild enthusiasm for doing deals, not only from the western side but also from hundreds of state corporations who saw the prising open of trade doors as the opening of a treasure trove. The attitude of many Chinese officials reflected that ancient outlook of the rulers of the Middle Kingdom; foreigners should think themselves richly blessed because they were permitted to trade with the celestial realm.

The notion that the world owed China a living and special generous terms should be extended by western business was not one that appealed to entrepreneurs whose only political and social concern was focused on the bottom line. Overseas Chinese, especially, were expected to scrap all normal rules of commercial acumen and extend open-handed terms to state corporations. In particular, members of the Chinese diaspora who had become wealthy abroad were looked at as philanthropists who had a duty to fund factories in their ancestral provinces.

As the initial enthusiasm began to wane, a more realistic approach to investment returned. The traditional idea of mutual benefit was once again embraced. Any businessman in China today will hear the phrase uttered again and again. It should be a welcome refrain. It means the state corporations and other bodies with whom they are signing agreements realise that a businessman has to make a profit.

The China Connection

Another phrase that is not so welcome in the new atmosphere is *guanxi* or connections. In modern parlance, this is an undefined linkage of close friends, old comrades, relatives, workmates and what in the west would be the Old Boy network.

If you are 'in the loop', to use another western expression, you are going to get special treatment. Your contract will be signed without great loss of time in negotiations. You will find raw materials provided and deadlines met. All problems will be smoothed over.

Based mostly on friendship and close relationships, *guanxi* also has a strong element of bribery. This is more in the form of luxury gifts, banquets and invitations to trips abroad than in hard cash. Those who cashed in most on connections in the past were high-ranking officials in state corporations, their family members and the children of top cadres in Beijing and provincial governments. They became known as 'fixers' who could cut through the smothering bonds of red tape that otherwise made doing deals so difficult.

Most of those who could extend the benefits of *guanxi* were Chinese and the beneficiaries were largely Overseas Chinese setting up shop in China.

After the student upheavals of the late 1980s, connections have been regarded with great suspicion and as part of the general corruption which sparked off the popular rising. But they are still invaluable, the invisible glue that holds together many of the business deals struck in China today.

Presents

Never offer cash. It is quite acceptable for foreigners doing business in China to take along small gifts to distribute to those they meet for discussions. But handing over money is crude, could be misunderstood and—in the worst possible scenario—could lead to an affronted Chinese official claiming some capitalistic westerner was attempting to corrupt him.

Such items as pen sets, solar calculators, transistor radios, Walkmans and other relatively cheap items are the favoured small presents. Cigarettes (any leading American brand) are always welcomed. I generally prefer taking books.

Just as anywhere else in the world, what you give depends on how well you know the recipient. If it is an official you have met on some former trip, you know whether he smokes and drinks, in which case a carton of cigarettes or a bottle of brandy may be

appropriate. In the case of new acquaintances, a degree of care is needed. While gifts may be appreciated, they should not be distributed in a way that can give offence.

The best way is to say, through your interpreter, that you appreciate greatly the help and hospitality you have received and would like very much your new friends in China to accept a small token of thanks. Mention also that if any of those present are ever in your town, you would very much like them to contact you so you can return their hospitality. This gesture will be greatly appreciated as a sign of friendship.

The ideal present is something tasteful. It should also be comparatively small so you can carry gifts in your baggage without too much trouble. Items like pens, desk sets and other mementos with your corporate logo are presents which are very suitable.

My own personal choice for close contacts are books. But here you have to know the person. Obviously, giving a book in English to someone who doesn't read the language is not an ideal solution. If you have met someone on an earlier trip who has been helpful and know he has a child, it touches the Chinese heart if on a return trip you bring a small token for the kid. It doesn't have to be big or expensive—western T-shirts are ideal but it will be a gesture that warms any relation.

In other words, good manners and politeness are universal.

WARNING: Do not take cameras to China to give as gifts. Chinese customs officials are paranoid about cameras. You have to list each one by make on entering the country and be prepared to show it to customs on the way out.

New Friends, Old Friends

Sometime on your first business trip to China, one of the cadres to whom you are talking will mention that you are welcome to the country as a 'new friend'. When you depart, the chances are you will be welcomed back in an elevated status.

'You came to our country as a new friend,' the ranking official will say as you prepare to leave his city or province. 'When you return, you will be an old friend.'

To Chinese, the difference is significant. A new friend, while welcome, is a person who comes to China on a visit. An old friend is someone who knows something of China.

As an 'old friend', one receives preferential treatment.

Open Cities

China's drive towards business modernisation was initially spearheaded by Guangzhou. Then Special Economic Zones (SEZs) were started, mostly clustered around Hongkong. The idea was that a symbiosis would grow between the world's most capitalistic city and the communist monolith. This idea worked; by 1988, more than two million people in Guangdong province worked in new factories owned by Hongkong companies which had invested a few miles away just over the provincial border. The Hongkong people had moved their plants over the border to take advantage of cheap labour, plentiful land and generous tax holidays offered by a government eager to attract manufacturers. These breaks more than offset the in-built burdens of doing business within a bureaucratic maze.

The SEZs were so successful that China later extended the welcome mat. Fourteen major coastal cities, from Zhangjiang on the Liuzhou Peninsula up to Dalian in Manchuria, were named as zones which officially welcomed foreigners. These blossomed commercially as each city strove to make more generous offers to attract business. The ground rules were laid down by the central government—ten-year tax holidays, permission to hire and fire staff and guarantees of being able to take out profits, to name a few—and bolstered by local efforts to make it easy for foreigners to set up shop.

These days, most of interior China is 'open' to business. In general, the further one gets from the coast, the more welcome the potential investor becomes. In go-ahead Qingdao and prosperous Xiamen, a manufacturer wanting to start a small television assembly plant might be greeted with a polite but distant handshake. Out in Anhui province or the backwaters of Guangxi, someone with a similar proposition would be hailed as an economic saviour.

The Guangzhou Trade Fair

When the Rattan Door of trade inched cautiously open in the early 1970s, the twice-yearly Guangzhou Trade Fair was China's main business window to the west. Today, the spring and autumn sessions of the fair still give merchants, especially newcomers, a vital and exciting overall picture of the national trading pattern. All 30 provinces put their goods on show. There are would-be wheelers and potential dealers from every industrial city in the land. Rug merchants from Central Asia rub shoulders with men who launch satellites from China's space bases, technicians demonstrate sophisticated medical electronic equipment and Sichuan officials demonstrate the intricate arts and crafts of mountain minority tribesmen. It is a place of great fascination and a week at the trade

At the twice-yearly trade fair in Guangzhou where China does a third of its foreign currency business, the wealth of the nation goes on show. Cadres admire a Shanghai-built ultra-light aircraft on sale for a fraction of the price of its western counterpart. In conjunction with American and European aircraft manufacturers, China now produces its own sophisticated passenger jets.

fair is equivalent to a couple of years studying China's business profile at a western university. It's also enormous fun.

Not only does the novice meet state traders from all over China and officials from the great ministries in Beijing, he also has the invaluable chance of having a drink with men and women who have been doing business with China for decades.

The old hands gather in the bar of the Dong Fang (East is Red) Hotel across the road from the glass-shrouded trade fair headquarters. There, they swap tales of the bad old days of the Cultural Revolution when import-export men from abroad were closely confined to the hotel, awakened at dawn every day by loudly-broadcast trumpets squealing the Maoist anthem (*The East is Red* which gave the hotel its name), then escorted across Liu Hua Road to do business through a guantlet of hysterical Red Guards screaming anti-western hate slogans. It was, the old timers say over a Zhu Jiang (Pearl River) lager, a lot of fun.

Today, these canny merchants who stayed on despite the rigours of doing business with fanatics are enjoying the pay-off. Today, they are the most respected of Old Friends. Listening to them, the new tramper of the Silk Road can pick up tips on doing business with China that the entire staff of the Harvard Business School would never dream of.

Working Hours

Officially, Chinese government offices and most companies work 8 a.m. to 5 p.m. six days a week. If you believe this, you'll believe anything. Be prepared for all business to stop abruptly at 11.30 a.m. or 4.30 p.m.—the cadres are called away for the most sacred business of all, lunch and dinner.

Officially, China has four holidays a year: New Year's Day (January 1), Labour Day (May 1), National Day (October 1) and the three-day break in late winter (depending on the lunar calendar) known as Spring Festival but celebrated with riotous good humour as Chinese New Year. Unofficially, many who try to do business with some slack Chinese concerns reckon that some Chinese bureaucrats and executives enjoy a 365-day-a-year holiday.

Let's Dance!

As China's doors hesitantly creaked open in the 1970s, some monstrous notions penetrated the land. One of these was that a sure sign of advanced thinking, liberal ideas and readiness to do business with the rest of the world was to have a disco in town.

Help me, boys! How many times have I been in some quiet backwater deep in the interior where, after dinner, the local mayor or party secretary has gripped me firmly in a hammerlock and

149

marched me determinedly to a darkened room in a hotel or meeting hall where a few tawdry coloured lights revolved and 1960s rock music blasted my eardrums. In the midst of this dim cacophony, a couple of girls would be coyly dancing together, watched by an approving mob of the local version of the Chamber of Commerce, factory supervisors and party functionaries, all eager to show their modernity.

Outside China, I went to a disco once. This was in Hongkong at the height of 'Saturday Night Fever' frenzy when I was enticed into one of these hellish places. I stayed 15 seconds. But in China, I must have been to a score of discos. While I am in no position to judge their quality, they seem to me sad, inappropriate places. Nobody there seems to know what to do or quite why they are present.

It's considered to be a sign of go-ahead local administration to have a disco and while officials seem to be as ignorant as I about what you do at a disco, it's just about compulsory for every village to have one and for the luckless foreign friend to be hauled into it.

Have fun.

Narrow Vision

China can be a narrow, blinkered place. Unless two people are assigned to the same work unit or have some other strong common bond, there seems little drive to meet people and make friends. Even within the same organisation or in the same factory, people do not mingle as they do in the west.

I have a good friend in the New China News Agency (known universally as Xinhua) and on a trip to Beijing I asked another Xinhua staffer how he was. The woman I asked looked at me in astonishment. He was in the English language section of the big organisation and she was in the Spanish-speaking section. So how could she possibly know anything about him? He was in a different section and therefore totally out of her ken.

You sometimes get the feeling that people who work in the same building but in different departments are as cut off from each other as you and I are removed from the august presence of Supreme Leader Deng.

This compartmentalism of Chinese life is not caused by the communist system, although the rigid bureaucracy of the system certainly reinforces the cultural isolation. If the other person doesn't have any direct impact on your life, why would you waste your time getting to know him?

In a Meeting

When you are told a business contact to whom you need to speak is 'in a meeting' the likelihood is that the poor soul is sitting down around a conference table with a dozen colleagues dutifully studying and analysing The Word as printed in that morning's *People's Daily*.

Political study meetings were virtually unknown for a few years, before coming back on the regular agenda in 1989 after the riotous upheavals which crippled the capital. Following the June 1989 suppression of pro-democracy demonstrations in Beijing, Shanghai, Chengdu and other cities, the political study meeting swiftly made an unwelcome reappearance.

What do they do at such gatherings? A good question, because westerners, naturally, are barred from such public soul-searching. Evidently, the technocrats, engineers, managers, foremen and other senior staff file into the room (usually the ghastly reception area) and are addressed by the party secretary of factory or work unit. He parrots the latest party line on events at home and abroad.

After studying the paper's version of what's happening in the world, the party secretary explains the situation and others are invited to comment. A few muttered words about the great wisdom and perspicacity being shown by the astute and talented party leaders in Beijing usually smooths proceedings and allows them to end in a mercifully short time.

Chapter Eight

LIVING IN CHINA

*To have done a thing oneself is better than
watching others do it;
To have made many mistakes in doing it
is better than simply doing it once.*

Most foreign companies classify living in China as a hardship
posting. In many ways, this is now untrue. In some other aspects, it
remains grimly evident. The newcomer who has the warm sheltering
arms of a large multinational company or the protective covering of
a diplomatic mission to provide the basics has little to complain

about. They have apartments on tap, their commissaries are well stocked with such exotic western delights as Scotch whisky and baked beans, and luxuries like telephones are already installed.

But just you try being a small businessman attempting to set up a one-man office in China. That's when the fun starts. Or try being a technician sent to a regional centre to advise on how best to use modern machinery. You are an exile cut off largely from many of the facilities that the rest of the world takes for granted.

Changing Times

Visitors going to China for the first time cannot begin to imagine what things were like a decade ago. Then, going to China may have been exciting. It was also like a swift trip backwards in a time machine to an era the rest of the world had forgotten. There is no point in dwelling on the esoteric miseries of those times. But for old business hands, progress in the past decade has been magical.

Fax machines, IDD telephone systems, copiers, business centres in hotels, access to foreign newspapers ... these are all recent developments. So when Old China Hands regale you with horror stories of the not-so-distant past, grin and bear it. You might even learn something.

Lifelines

One piece of advice for any businessman, student, adviser or Foreign Friend who is to be stationed away from the largest cities on the tourist track: take plenty to read and arrange before you go to China for a lifeline with friends outside the country to send you a steady supply of books. This is probably the best opportunity you will ever have to catch up on reading the classics; there is precious little else to do in many of the backwoods towns.

Whenever I go to China, I am accompanied by one of my most prized possessions. This is a small Sony shortwave radio, the size of a paperback novel. Using normal batteries obtainable anywhere, this electronic wonder plugs me into the outside world. During long northern nights when darkness plunges most of the nation into silence like a mausoleum, I whip out the antenna and am in contact with the world. This machine has a 'seek' command that scans all shortwave and medium-wave frequencies. After a couple of days, you can pick up Voice of America, Radio Australia, Radio Japan, Radio Moscow or stations broadcasting in German, Spanish, Indonesian, French, Hindi or a score of other tongues.

The best of this plethora of news and views of the airways is the British Broadcasting Corporation's magnificent World Service. This has news on the hour, interviews with topical figures, chat shows, book reviews and in-depth research profiles on top news items of the day. Many a long, icy night I have spent huddled under the down cover of a rural guesthouse bed with my radio tuned to distant London as I awaited the dawn.

You can also tune in to Radio Beijing and hear the news according to the Forbidden City. This often gives a quaint viewpoint on the world. More usefully, you can spend the insomniac hours of the night with your ears glued to the first-class Chinese language classes offered by many English-language broadcasts. I have always found Radio Australia—which sends a very strong signal to Northern China—to be the best of these. But Radio Beijing's excellent programme 'Follow Me!' which teaches an estimated 100 million people daily how to speak English is also well worth listening to.

Ironically, although it is impossible to buy English language newspapers in many areas of China, I often arrive back in my hometown of Hongkong (where there are 68 daily newspapers and the best communications links on earth) with a better grasp of global news and current events than many of my newspaper colleagues. This is because I have spent up to eight hours a night listening to radio stations broadcasting from every continent on earth.

Staying in Touch

A decade ago, when the foreigner entered China he strode nervously into an information vacuum. There were the local newspapers, all tightly controlled by the propaganda department of the party, and radio and television under a similar vice-like grip. All were in the national tongue, of course, with no Cantonese broadcasts even in the great southern metropolis of Guangzhou. The only reading matter were dreary publications like *China Reconstructs* and similar publications in a variety of languages which endlessly proclaimed in breathless prose the great strides being made under the wise leadership of the regime.

As with so many other aspects of Chinese life, things have, happily, changed. Now, in tourist hotels in big cities, you can buy international news magazines, a selection of paperbacks, guide books and novels. In big cities like Beijing, Shanghai and Guangzhou, that morning's Hongkong newspapers are on the stands by the time you are heading for the bar for a 5 p.m. glass of Baiyuan beer.

The English language *China Daily* is put out by the Central Government in Beijing and, naturally enough, follows the Party line. It also contains readable and topical features. The *Daily* (pronounced *Zhongguo Ribao* in Putonghua) is well worth reading, if only to get a look at the world through an official Chinese perspective.

Hold the Mei-you

One of the first phrases foreigners in China come to know and hate is *mei-you*. Intoned normally in a high-pitched whine, it means, literally, 'don't have'. It can also mean, depending on pronunciation, time of day, the bad humour of the shop assistant or the indifference of the clerk, anything from 'It's too much trouble' or 'Don't bother me with your problems' or, simply, 'beat it'.

Mei-you ... it's the song of modern China.

You want a cold bottle of beer in a hotel and you approach the

barman who is busy watching television. '*Mei-you*.'

You try to book a ticket on an aircraft at a CITS office and the bureaucrat is reading the paper. '*Mei-you*.'

A cash customer is eager to buy a sweater in a state-run shop and the size he wants is not easy to hand on the counter. '*Mei-you*.'

You try to board a taxi when the driver doesn't feel like driving. '*Mei-you*.'

Chances are, it will be the first word with which you become fully proficient. It covers every eventuality in which the foreigner finds himself. If in doubt, shrug, turn away and mutter '*mei-you*'.

It's the answer for everything.

A few years ago, a disgruntled young American at a language university in Beijing became so irate at the continual chant that greeted his every request that he asked a friend in Hongkong to have a few hundred T-shirts printed. They bore an outline of the Great Wall overprinted with the English slogan: 'China—Hold the *mei-you*.' No Chinese could understand the motto but the shirts became an instant success with Beijing's growing foreign community, all of whom had suffered an overdose of '*mei-you*'.

Pace

One of the frustrations for a foreigner living in China is the pace at which people move. Generally, they resemble a snail on holiday. This is visibly apparent at service desks in government offices where as a matter of face the staff make the customers wait—just to let them know who is boss. The painful, slow pace of work in what in the west would be the public service would make the slackest, most bloody-minded British socialist look like an Olympic sprinter dosed with steroids.

The difference is obvious in the increasing number of shops run by private enterprise. Here service is swift and friendly, staff are eager to help, keen to get out the goods and assist you to try on clothing.

The contrast is stark.

Shopping

Going shopping for residents of China is a lot different than for visitors. Tourists want to pick up bargain-priced antiques or mementos of their trip. Residents have to buy their daily necessities.

Until just a few years ago, if you lived in China you ate what was on sale at local markets. You had FEC of course, so you could go to the Friendship Stores and purchase things like mackerel in tomato sauce. Big deal. There was nothing else.

In the big cities, this is no longer the case. The large foreign-run hotels in places where there are sizeable foreign communities have delicatessens where French bread, American chocolates and fresh-made German sausages are available.

In Beijing, the Lido Holiday Inn has nine butchers making an enormous array of smoked meats, sausages and *wursts* that could come from a Bavarian farmyard. This Teutonic gastronomic lifeline connects to every city in North China with German communities. Up in the Mongolian steel city of Baotou, German technicians look forward to the plane from Beijing that comes bearing *bratwurst*.

Hongkong supermarkets have now opened branches in Beijing; similar organisations selling western groceries and basic necessities can be found in a few other big cities. Elsewhere, you either shop at Chinese stores or go without.

Arts and Crafts

The visitor sometimes asks himself, where is the legacy of 5000 years of culture? Where are the arts and crafts on which China so endlessly prides herself? Often, this is a very good question to which no logical or easy answer can be found.

Take the city of Chaozhou, old cultural centre of the wealthy Shantou region on the Guangdong coast. This district prides itself intensely on its ceramic heritage. Famed also for brocade and lacquer work, it is centre of a region with a distinguished history of local crafts. Every tour guide and public official discourses at length on the cultural heritage of the region. Having listened to such talk for a couple of hours over lunch, now venture out onto the street of this once great port (heavy siltage of the river now places it far inland) and attempt to buy something. Good luck.

The shops are full, that is true. The shelves are stocked with modern manufactured cloth, plastic buckets, imitation leather jackets and brightly coloured cheap clothing.

Where is the gold embroidery? A shrug. '*Mei-you.*'

The ceramics for which you are famed? '*Mei-you.*'

The paintings? '*Mei-you.*'

Or try Shandong. You've heard of Shandong silk? Of course. It's renowned. I have tramped for hours around the streets of the provincial capital, Jinan, along the 10-kilometre circumference of the park where the city walls and moat once stood and through miles of downtown streets.

Shandong silk? '*Mei-you.*'

What's that brilliant scarf? That's silk, right enough, but it's imported from Turkey!

Where can you buy Shandong silk?

Try the Friendship Store in Beijing.

In Taiyuan, in historic Shanxi, the biggest antique shop boasted three carpets which had been there for years and couldn't be disturbed because junky plastic goods had been piled atop them for a decade.

In Hangzhou, home of the Southern Song dynasty which made the city a glorious artistic imperial capital, there are some nice ceramics to be found. But the shop shuts on the dot of dusk so staff can collapse after a weary day spent reading the papers and dozing.

Shopping in official China can be a disappointing business.

The Profit Motive Rears Its Welcome Head

Increasingly, small family businesses are opening in China to take advantage of the yawning commercial opportunities created by the slothful incompetence of official outlets. These are places normally located close to private enterprise restaurants in areas where tourists are likely to stroll.

The difference between the eager, friendly service one encounters here and the idle, couldn't-care-less attitude that is universal in state-run enterprises provides a stark lesson in economics. The benefits of the profit motive would be obvious to the ghost of Mao Zedong.

Stacked with cheap ceramics, these shops, like one I found in friendly Xiamen, often contain a few old pieces. Spend a few minutes browsing. Admire what you want. Ignore what you can find back home.

Picking the Baddies

It started a couple of years ago in Xian where a go-ahead shop manager decided to do something about his staff. He instituted a 'Nominate the Most Lazy Shop Assistant' contest. Customers were asked to write down the most useless, rudest and incompetent worker in the store and slip their selections into a locked ballot box. More people voted in this election than in picking the Party General Secretary in Beijing. It unveiled a near-universal discontent with the way the shop was run. When the votes were toted up, the least popular staff members were named and their portraits pinned up on the store's entrance hall. They improved their performance.

The idea caught on and one can now write in complaints in many stores throughout the country. Needless to say, I am an enthusiastic voter in these polls. There are thousands of candidates from whom to pick.

Striking a Deal

Unlike the vibrant Chinese communities abroad, there is little bargaining in shops in China. In the state-run enterprises, prices are fixed. Things are much freer and easier, and pleasant, in the increasing number of private enterprise shops. Here, the natural Chinese genius for making a deal, striking a bargain, is once more flourishing.

My rule of thumb is to offer a quarter of the price the shopkeeper demands. This gives plenty of leeway for both sides to come to an agreement.

Always smile. Set a pleasant tone. Have a look around a shop and if you spy a teapot without which you cannot possibly live, pick up another item and ask the price.

The shopkeeper will look at you, sizing up your IQ and wallet. If he thinks the first is suitably small and the latter disgustingly fat, he will make an inflated suggestion.

'One hundred yuan,' he might say.

I slap my hand to my forehead, reel backwards in shock and outrage and, still smiling, protest. 'You must be the richest man in all Jiangsu province,' or wherever I might be. 'I am a poor worker, exploited by the capitalists.'

If you're with a Chinese friend, this translation will bring a hearty grin. There will be a bit of conversation; where are you from, is this your first time in China, etc.

Then you make a counter offer for the item you do not want.
'Thirty yuan.'

It is the shopkeeper's turn to loudly lament and proclaim his poverty. Down he comes to RMB70. You weep. You throw your hands in the air. How about if you pay in Hongkong dollars? you query. Or American dollars?

The shopkeeper takes this bait like a hammerhead shark in a feeding frenzy. So, roughly calculating, you offer a red Hongkong $100 note. At the official rate of exchange, this is about RMB50 worth about RMB85 on the black market. You don't want to be too greedy so you tell the shopkeeper you will buy two items for HK$100. Done! he says.

But not what you were bargaining over, you say. Then you point to the teapot that you *really* want to buy and, having established the value of the Hongkong dollar, start serious negotiations.

A while ago, in the old port city of Shantou, I bought a marvellous large glazed porcelain vase for the equivalent of US$4. I was so stunned by the price asked that I didn't even bother to negotiate. The shopkeeper in turn was so surprised not to have a pleasurable and lengthy argument over the price that he pointed out to me an invisible flaw in the vase. We were both happy.

Gifts

When you're onto a good thing, stick with it. Years ago, I discovered the Friendship Store in Shanghai, down near the Bund close to the river end of Nanjing Road. You can't miss it. Having been frustrated on so many trips trying to buy small presents, it was with some joy that I discovered this huge and cavernous department store stocked with an enormous array of arts, crafts and silks.

What caused my enthusiasm to soar even higher was the plump and jolly lady who staffed the silk counter where they accepted foreign credit cards. I swiftly instituted a system with her that works to this day.

Get to Shanghai, unpack my computer and head downtown. Into the Friendship Store (one of the few that deserves to bear the name) and up to the third floor to the silk lady. '*Ni hao!*' we grin at each other. I then dash down the counter pointing to a dozen or so bolts of different silk. She whips them out and I depart, leaving her my credit card.

Over the road and around the corner to the dim and dusty old bar of the Peace Hotel. A quick Qingdao beer, then back to the store. When I return, the silks are all cut into three-metre lengths and my bill is waiting to be signed. 'Many thanks,' I say, bidding her farewell and striding out, deeply satisfied. Here I have just completed my Christmas shopping in 60 seconds, having bought dress lengths of silk for four sisters, a mother-in-law, a daughter and assorted friends in various countries.

But do not tarry in the Shanghai treasure house. It is stocked with extremely tempting goodies. One trip, I took an English couple with me and instead of my normal blinding 60-second shopping foray we had to hang around while the wife admired carved wooden horses, lacquer ware, gold rings inlaid with semi-precious stones and other items. I got talking to the fellow who runs the carpet section and when I emerged from the shop I was the proud owner of a silken prayer rug woven by Turkic tribesmen out in far Xinjiang province. At US$2600, it was a pricey visit. But a couple of years later, a friend who is knowledgeable about such matters spotted the rug and raved about it. Apparently, I had got a bargain. I still prefer the 60-second forays.

Money

A few years ago, I was in a restaurant in Zhengzhou, capital of historic old Henan where the Yellow River comes flooding out onto the North China Plain, and the talk moved to the inevitable subject of the future of Hongkong.

Mrs Thatcher had just been up to Beijing (where Comrade Deng

Living in China means you will be expected to host banquets for Chinese business contacts who have shown you hospitality. The very worst thing a foreigner could do is get a reputation as a bad host.

Xiaoping enquired of an aide 'Who is this dumb woman?') to negotiate the pact which sealed the future of the colony and consigned its six million people unwillingly to a political future within China.

What did I think of the agreement? party leaders asked.

In answer, I reached into my hip pocket, got my wallet and extracted a Hongkong $100 bill.

'The people will resolutely follow the red banner of Hongkong,' I said, waving the scarlet note aloft.

There was much laughter all round and we had another flask of the famed Dujiang wine, a particularly noxious brew with heady effects.

On a more serious note, having a few Hongkong $100 notes in your pocket when shopping in China can be a lot of use.

Do not change money with street black marketeers—that's illegal —but you *can* legally spend Hongkong money in shops. So if you

163

are bargaining in a free enterprise shop and make offers to buy in Hongkong currency, you often get extremely good prices.

The familiar red notes are devoutly admired throughout China.

Sex

In 1984, the late Dr Ma Haide had to take China's doctors back to school. The medicos had to learn the symptoms of diseases that doctors in China had not had to treat for a generation.

With the opening of the bamboo curtain and swarms of tourists going to China, the inevitable had happened. Sex had reared its ugly head and the result was the re-appearance of venereal disease. So Dr Ma, as American-born as George Hatem in Buffalo, New York, had to instruct Chinese doctors what to look for if patients went to them with a problem. Ironically, it was Ma Haide who after 1949 had led the medical drive that eliminated the widespread prostitution in cities such as Shanghai and which, to all intents, had wiped out VD in China.

The new liberalism which accompanied the advent of foreigners and wealthy Overseas Chinese saw a reversal from the strident puritanical attitude that ruled Chinese morals when Mao Zedong was alive. Boy met girl and the result sooner or later was love.

This did not go down well with many of the Old Guard. Lusty as they may have been themselves in their revolutionary youth a half century earlier, they were not keen to see sex blossoming in public places like the park in the Bund in Shanghai. To stamp out such practices as kissing in public (and the other shameful appurtenances of what was seen as western moral corruption), a campaign was launched against 'bourgeois pollution'. It created a lot of headlines but didn't do much to stop people doing what came naturally.

Silver Bullets

When the idealistic communists took power in 1949, they were appalled by the immensity of the problems facing them. They were determined to change many things and close to the top of their list of essential moves was to stamp out prostitution.

This was not only on moral grounds. There were also ideological reasons. For centuries, many Chinese women and girls had been casually sold into concubinage or sexual slavery. They were treated not so much as human beings but as commodities. The communists were determined to stamp out the trade in women; most of the soldiers of the Red Army were peasants and it was peasant women who were sold when the crops failed.

In Shanghai, estimates were that one house in 12 was a brothel. They were staffed by many thousands of women and girls, some of whom had been sold by their families to pay for rice so brothers and sisters might live. Beneath the foreign image of the silken glamour of Shanghai's glittering nightlife, there was desperation and degradation.

The Reds rounded up the whores—many of them forced into the life by gangsters—and shipped them off to re-education camp. They were treated for VD and taught a trade that could support them, and thus provided with a medical and economic foundation for a new life. The pimps were lucky if they went to prison; most were shot.

'Silver bullets' was what the communists called prostitutes on the grounds that their temptations could be used as ammunition against the new regime.

Good-time Girls

Prostitution has reappeared in China despite all the moral preachings of party and government. A factory girl earns RMB100 a month, if she's lucky. Widespread reports in western newspapers make it plain that eager freelancers can make that much and a lot more in an illicit engagement with an Overseas Chinese or foreigner.

The hottest spots for prostitutes are around the big hotels in tourist cities like Shanghai and Guangzhou. Some of the bars that have appeared suddenly like mushrooms in a spring rain in many cities are said to be houses of assignation. You can get a lot more than a beer there.

For non-Chinese foreigners, dallying with commercial sex can be hazardous. Every hotel room in China has a warning notice listing regulations, one of which is that prostitution is banned. There have been stories about hotel staff alerting police to a foreigner taking a whore to his room; and of the Public Security Bureau knocking on the door before the customer could get his pants off.

There's no doubt prostitutes are active again in China. But there is none of the coercion and outright slavery that filled the brothels of Shanghai in the bad old days.

Falling in Love

It happens every day. Usually, there are problems, often serious. Some Chinese who have had the misfortune to fall in love with a foreigner in recent years have been banished to some remote interior city. Others have been refused permission to leave the country when their spouse departed. This led in one case to a fiery Frenchwoman staging a lay-down protest outside the Chinese embassy in Paris, threatening to have her baby on the pavement if her husband was not allowed to join her. He was. As with so many other aspects of China, things are loosening up, getting easier.

It is often difficult for westerners to get to know locals of the opposite sex. There is ingrained prejudice and a large degree of ignorance about the outside world. While many young Chinese men and women would like nothing better than to date a foreigner, they have to overcome opposition from relatives and incessant joshing from friends.

Getting to know each other can be tricky. Usually, the visitor to China will meet people in the travel industry or associated business such as shops. Businessmen may meet colleagues or people who work in similar industries but the opportunity for friendships to be formed are restricted. First of all, there is often the language barrier.

More imposing is the cultural hurdle. Despite the easing of bans on meeting foreigners and the general liberalisation of morals, China is still, by western standards, a staid and proper society. There is very little casual sex. It happens, of course, but much more rarely than in American, European or Australian societies.

For those who live in China, romance can and does bloom.

Watch Those Hands

Respect Chinese women. Take care when you are dealing with waitresses and other service staff that you do not mistakenly insult them by taking perceived sexual advantage.

When you are in a modern western-managed hotel and a slinky, enormously sexy girl glides past in a high-cut *cheongsam*, do not make a mistake and think she is anything but a waitress. You'll be very sorry if you do.

A drunken, lonely and amorous Dutchman once patted a waitress on her shapely bottom in a Guangzhou hotel lounge. She didn't say anything but walked out of the room. Within 10 minutes, she was back, accompanied by two burly hotel security guards who in China are often unofficial representatives of the local Public Security Bureau. They were carrying his bags. Packed.

'You are leaving China on the next train,' the dumbfounded Hollander was told. He was marched out of the hotel, put in a taxi, given his train ticket, directed to the station and told not to return.

Serves him right ...

Costs

China may be a poor country. This does not mean it is a cheap one. Living in China can be as expensive as anywhere in the world. Decent apartments are virtually impossible to obtain for most foreigners so home is likely to be a permanent hotel room or a serviced flat in an apartment tower next to a foreign-run hotel.

Cheap they are not.

But living in a hotel service block is the most viable choice for anyone who does not have quarters provided by employer or the local Chinese organisation to which he is attached. Costs at the China Hotel in Guangzhou are US$60 a night for a long-term stay of three months or more. Apartments in the tower block adjoining the hotel range from US$2000 a month for a 75 square metres room to US$6700 per month for a three-bedroom apartment measuring 185 square metres. In Beijing, add another 30 per cent to these costs. Such accommodation comes with everything supplied.

Trying to get such services as water, garbage collection and staff privately can be a nightmare, even for Overseas Chinese who speak fluent Putonghua. For a foreigner, the maze of horrors through which one has to go to get a telephone connected is a bureaucratic atrocity. In a hotel service apartment, most of your problems of setting up house are solved.

Some people who know they are going to be based in China for a couple of years have the romantic notion of renting a *wutung*, living off a lane in one of the old traditional houses. This inevitably turns out to be more expensive than a hotel apartment and no matter how enthusiastically the idea is grasped at the start, the grim realities of getting anything done soon cause the experiment to be regretted.

On the other hand, in hotels where large numbers of students, foreign experts and long-term businessmen are quartered, there develops a warm, friendly community spirit. Such a place is the Friendship Hotel in Beijing where many overseas journalists who work in Radio Beijing are based, as are large contingents of Third World graduate students. It's a merry place, despite the crumbling condition of the rambling old building, and the decrepit and tawdry bar has a happy club-like atmosphere. There is a feeling of camaraderie; I suppose inmates on Devil's Island were also matey with each other.

Come Over For Dinner

In Beijing, there are four major compounds where diplomats, journalists, permanent resident businessmen and others who live in the city for lengthy postings occupy large but not-too-comfortable apartments. Naturally, these have high walls around them. Nobody seems quite sure if they are designed to keep intruders out or to pen the foreigners in.

What invariably causes rage and disgust to foreign residents is the discovery that their Chinese friends cannot come and visit them. If they try, they will be stopped at the gates by armed guards. The People's Armed Police are supposedly stationed at the compound gates to protect the inhabitants. From what, I've never learned.

Most Chinese will skilfully avoid an invitation to your home. Even with a printed invitation to show the haughty guard, they will be questioned and have their names taken down. In times of political uncertainty, anyone going to see a foreigner (especially a newsman or diplomat) is likely to have to explain why. It's best for Chinese not to come to the attention of the authorities.

So if you want to meet a friend, it's best to go for dinner in a restaurant. This may seem outrageous to newcomers. To Chinese, it is, sadly, a fact of life.

On Your Bike

One of the first purchases a foreigner who has gone to live in China is likely to make is a Seagull bicycle. This is the gift that China gave to President Bush when he visited Beijing and it was splendidly appropriate. The great bulk of people use bicycles for commuting and getting about their cities.

It's an enjoyable way of experiencing the cities. It's also eminently sensible and gives a foreigner a chance to see the sights through Chinese eyes. Bikes can be hired through most hotel concierge desks and pedalling about town is fun.

Incidentally, doctors stress to me that the reason China has such a low incidence of heart disease can largely be linked to the life-long regular exercise people get pedalling to school and work and the marketplace. Add this to a healthy diet and the long life enjoyed by most people is explained despite the country's primitive medical infrastructure.

Keeping Fit

In many larger cities, foreign-run hotels now operate fitness and health centres. These come equipped with exercise machines, weights and saunas, and staffed by keep-fit experts and aerobics instructors. With little else to do in the evenings, such centres are busy.

While jogging in China has not reached the craze levels of the western world, it is still a common sight to see people pounding along pavements in the early light of dawn.

Much more common is to see people of all ages out under the willow trees and at lakesides carrying out the strict, patterned movements of *tai chi* exercises. For anyone living in China, it is easy to find an instructor. Simply join the local *tai chi* group which every morning gathers to do their exercises near where you live.

If you can't speak Chinese, ask a friend to go with you the first morning to explain who you are and that you want to take part in the exercises. You'll be shyly but warmly welcomed. Then just follow the leader as the group goes through the sedate movements of this ancient martial arts discipline.

You'll find *tai chi* relaxing as well as stimulating and although the pace is slow and easy, the various exercises stretch muscles and tone up all parts of the body.

Quality of Life

So what's it like to live in China? Opinions vary. There is, however, universal agreement that it is now a lot more pleasant, relaxed and comfortable than a decade ago or even three years ago. The turmoil and clampdown of 1989 has not affected to any extent the foreign community. Panicky westerners fled Beijing in droves when the tanks rumbled into Tiananmen. There was no reason to leave.

Daily life can still be difficult. In Beijing, there is the International School. The standards of this institution are patchy. Many of the children, particularly those of Third World diplomats, are spoiled juvenile delinquents whose bottoms would do well to become acquainted with a rattan cane.

If you want lively entertainment, rock 'n' roll, wild parties, a wide variety of good, affordable restaurants, superb wines and opportunities to meet the opposite sex, don't go to live in China.

In most towns, pollution is a serious problem. This is largely caused by the habit of burning packed bricks of coal dust in the home. The air is gritty. Diesel fumes make the eyes weep. Most Chinese cities give little thought to urban beautification and even in the middle of showcase Beijing, outside splendid joint venture hotels that cost US$100 million, you are liable to find stretches of potholed pavements that look like Upper Volta on a bad day.

Changing times have brought immense improvement. High technology has played a part in this. Take the invention of the VCR. In most cities, foreign residents get films sent in from their head offices at home and enthusiastic bands of cassette swappers exchange movies. This gives something to do in the drabness of the long and featureless nights.

In most cities where there are foreign residents, permanent or temporary, one of the local hotels has been selected as the local bar where people gather. A friendly club-like atmosphere soon develops. German friends liken this to the *stammsicht* tradition in their homeland where one table in a bar is reserved for regulars. A fresh face is always welcome and if you go into a bar in China and see a bunch of fellows drinking together, just ask if they live in the city. They will delight in welcoming you into their circle and there's no better way to get an idea of how a city works and what it is like than

to sit down over a half-dozen beers with people who have been based there for a few years.

Entertainment

Make your own. In big foreign hotels, television often offers in-house movies that you probably saw on an aircraft five years ago. Chinese TV is, naturally, in Chinese. You can go out to the movies, first checking that the show has English subtitles. But one visit to a Chinese cinema where people spit, eat and smoke throughout the show is probably enough to put you off a return trip.

Chinese western music, almost always classical, is excellent. The standard of musicians is among the best in the world. But getting concert tickets is normally very difficult.

Ask your hotel or friends to let you know about performances of local acrobatic or magic troupes. They are astonishing, without doubt the best on earth.

Go once to a Chinese opera, for the experience. To the western ear, Chinese opera is a dreadful cacophony. To the unskilled eye, the movements of the colourfully adorned performers are scenic but their roles are incomprehensible.

It is wonderful light entertainment, however, compared to Tibetan opera. A good friend took me along to one of these highland cultural performances one night, and in about a century, I will start to think of forgiving him. Tibetan culture consists of a performer with a voice that could cut marble singing at 100 decibels to one note hovering in the region of high C. This lasts for three or four hours, when he departs, to be replaced by his identical twin who does likewise. Then a stream of other Tibetans, deities, goddesses, mountain herdsmen, feudal barons and people miraculously transformed into birds traipse across the stage, all of them bellowing at the top of their voices with amplification loud enough to wake up the monks in the Potala Palace, 3700 kilometres away.

I'm told this is very cultural. Enjoy.

Servants

If your company is paying for a servant, or if you can afford to pay RMB50 a month out of your own pocket, you can enjoy a holiday from the heavy housework while you live in China. In Beijing, the Personnel Service Corporation handles all applications and the person you get to work in your home is the one they assign to you. This could be marvellous or it could turn out to be less than fortuitous. It's all in the luck of the draw. There are similar arrangements in other cities.

It is difficult to come to some informal agreement to get someone to work for you. The language barrier is one obvious problem, shyness is another, but the major problem is finding some official to give a Chinese permission to work in close proximity to foreigners in a private arrangement.

In the capital and other big cities with large permanent foreign populations, there are few problems. You apply to the personnel department and in the fullness of time, a servant will turn up. Make sure in the initial interview that both of you know what duties are expected.

Drugs

The communists regard China as having been historically a victim of narcotics forced on the nation by outsiders. There is much justification for this view. It was a bunch of grasping Scots and English drug peddlars who insisted on breaking Qing laws by running drugs into China that sparked off the First Opium War. The result was the seizure of Hongkong Island by the British and the forcible opening of treaty ports up and down the coast. This humiliation of Chinese sovereignty (albeit the regime was Manchu) is still a prickly subject.

When the communists came to power, one of the first proclamations they made was that the use of narcotics had to stop. They gave fair warning. In six months, the party said, anyone found smoking, possessing, growing, trafficking or dealing in opium or any of its derivatives would be punished. The Chinese had heard many such threats before. For six months, nothing was done.

Then the communists proved themselves as good as their word. Six months to the day after the warning was given, police throughout the country swooped. Drug runners were lined up and shot.

They still are. With the opening of China, some greedy and foolish people have attempted to use Chinese airports as staging posts to smuggle drugs to the west. One favourite route is to pick up heroin in Bangkok and fly to China. There the tourist spends a couple of days and then flies on to the United States. Because customs officials know that drugs are virtually unknown in China, checks for narcotics on flights arriving from China tend to be casual. They are far less stringent than on flights arriving direct from Thailand, for example.

The profits of drug running in China are slim. If caught, traffickers are dealt with in a speedy fashion. It's arrest one day, up in court the next and that afternoon the drug runner has a date with the executioner in the local football stadium. There, with a placard around his neck detailing his crime, he gets a bullet in the brain in front of a crowd of spectators.

No westerner has yet been executed simply because none has been caught smuggling drugs. The best anyone caught with drugs in China can expect is a lengthy prison sentence, at least 10 years in jail, to ponder the wisdom of his ways. You have been warned.

Law and Order

China is a peaceable country. Even at the height of the pro-democracy struggle in the spring and summer of 1989, tourists were safe throughout the land.

There is no mugging. There is little theft. I feel no qualms about leaving camera gear worth thousands of dollars and wallets full of cash in hotel rooms anywhere in the country. I have never been threatened anywhere in China. Nobody I know has ever been robbed or had anything stolen.

This is not to say there is no crime in China. Read the local papers and you will see accounts of murder, rape, assault and personal crimes the same as anywhere in the world. Justice in China is swift and punishment certain. Robbers and rapists are shot. Murderers are almost invariably executed. The death penalty is also imposed for economic crimes against the state, for large-scale corruption and organised theft from state corporations.

Civil libertarians might protest these drastic measures but for tourists, at least, they result in a country which is safe to visit. Women can walk safely after dark in any Chinese city. If you get lost, any policeman will be glad to help you.

No Second Chance

The big campaign to crack down on civil crime is said to have started in 1983 after Deng Xiaoping and other party leaders witnessed a murder during their annual summer retreat to the northern beach resort of Beihaidei. Whatever the reason, after a period of relative leniency, the death penalty was swiftly reintroduced throughout the country for crimes of violence.

A few months after this began, I was down in rural Guangdong where one day I was sitting on a bus beside a local party cadre who was attached to the People's Armed Police. How was the law and order campaign going, I enquired. Did the death penalty, widely publicised and with executions being attended by many thousands of people, act as a deterrent?

He thought for a moment.

'Well,' he said finally. 'I suppose it is a deterrent. But I'll tell you one thing. We don't get any second offenders.'

Don't get the idea that the death penalty is some horrible communist custom; all Chinese societies take a tough view on crime and punishment and capital sentences are in the traditional mould.

Chapter Nine

CUISINE

Hot oil or bitter cabbage—
every man to his own taste.

Viands have various flavours.
What pleases the palate is good.

Much of Chinese daily life revolves around food. There is an old saying that while other people eat to live, the Chinese live to eat. There is a lot of truth in this truism. Simply to bid someone good morning in Cantonese, you say '*Jo saan.*' Literally, this means

'Have you taken rice?'

The delights of the table go back beyond Confucius. A gourmet himself, the great philosopher wrote glowingly of the importance of food. Through the ages, poets, emperors and warriors were expected to be connoisseurs of fine dining. The dinner table was one of the elegant highlights of a gentleman's or noble's existence and he was expected to be able to discourse knowledgeably on food, its history and preparation.

A Few Examples

One of the many hundreds of dishes attributed to a poet is that distinctive Hangzhou speciality, **Dong Po Pork**. The tale goes that the famed writer and calligrapher of the Northern Song, Su Dong Po, was in charge of dredging the jewel of the area, the willow-fringed West Lake. He had a work force of 200,000 men and, to encourage them to toil mightily, he ordered an army of chefs to prepare hearty dishes of fat pork casseroled in the sweet rice wine of nearby Shaoxing. The city still delights in this 1000-year-old dish.

Military men were also expected to be familiar with kitchen techniques when they had done with the battlefield for military tactics. **General T'so's Chicken** recalls the campaigns of a fiery general who loved his chickens fried in hot red chillies.

Mandarins bequeathed to China many delicacies because rulers of the state were expected also to be gourmets and scholars as well as administrators. But, naturally, most of the great dishes of China can be traced back to the grassroots, to the peasant villages where the bulk of the people always lived.

Among the best-known is **Beggar's Chicken**. There is fierce provincial and regional rivalry over where this aromatic dish originated with chefs in Jiangsu, Fujian, Anhui and Zhejiang all arguing heatedly that it was first accidentally baked in their home areas. While this is a lively way in which to spend an hour over a flask of Shaoxing wine, it doesn't really matter.

The legend is the same everywhere. A poor landless peasant was starving and as he roamed the countryside looking for edible roots or anything else to stave off hunger, he stumbled across a plump chicken. Within seconds, he had grasped the bird and wrung its neck. Eagerly, he lit a fire by the side of a stream and as the wood burned down to hot coals, he plucked the fowl.

Suddenly, the sound of horse hooves could be heard. Riding up came the local noble with an entourage of swordsmen. To be found with the stolen bird would mean death so the wily peasant swiftly plunged into the stream, scooped up mud and weeds growing on the bank and plastered them around the bird. He threw the ball of clay onto the fire.

The noble reined in his horse. What are you doing, he asked the peasant. Making bricks, sire, came the answer, pointing to the mud in the flames. On rode the horsemen.

As soon as they were safely out of sight, the beggar used sticks to pull the hardened clay out of the glowing coals. Using a stone, he broke the container and was enveloped in a magical cloud of heavenly steam. The weeds he had so hurriedly plucked were wild herbs and lotus leaves and they had cooked inside the sealed clay with the chicken. Today, that same feast can be enjoyed in many regions of coastal China. It is one of the true wonders of Chinese gastronomy.

Wherever you eat it, your local dinner companions will tell you it originated near by. Nod in agreement and reach for some more of this succulent, juicy fowl and give thanks to the beggar of old.

The Four Regions

Just about every cookbook you read on China divides the nation into four culinary regions. There is justification for this. It's also incorrect. It ignores the huge variety of regional cuisines that are a matter of great local culinary patriotism in every corner of the land. We won't get into that argument here. There are more than 19,000 Chinese cookbooks in print that deal with the subject in depth.

The four basic gastronomic areas widely recognised by gourmets are the cuisines of Canton, Shanghai, Sichuan and Beijing.

Cantonese

The culinary capital of the nation is without a doubt the great southern city of Guangzhou, a citadel of magnificent dining for more than 1000 years and an area with a distinctive elegance in eating.

The secret in Cantonese cooking is freshness and lightness. Live prawns and vegetables picked from the market gardens that morning are steamed, simply and swiftly. The natural juices and taste of the ingredients stand by themselves without benefit of sauces, salt, sugar or any other additives. On a culinary map, what is known as 'Cantonese' food would cover the southeastern corner of the country. But within this area there is an enormous range of various local cuisines. Each hamlet has its own speciality and way of cooking and preparing food. And there are many strongly distinctive regional cuisines within the Cantonese food family.

The *dim sum* taken to the world by southern Chinese is a Cantonese custom. What you've had overseas is a pallid imitation. There is nothing else on earth that can compare with a crowded *dim sum* palace on a busy holiday morning. The extended family is there. All of them, three or four generations. People shout for different blends of tea. Serving trolleys roll through the crowded tables with aged crones to shapely young girls screeching out their wares. The sound crashes off the walls. In a good *dim sum* restaurant, it sounds as though World War III is being waged.

To Cantonese, the sound and the fury are almost as important as the food. Those heavenly prawns wrapped in translucent pastry, narrow baby pork ribs marinated in garlic, chicken feet steamed for hours in ginger and beef balls aromatic with coriander … the dishes arrive in endless profusion.

For the treat of a lifetime, when in Guangzhou beg your hotel to make reservations for you to have breakfast at the Panxi teahouse. This is the premier Chinese teahouse on earth, set amid courtyards, ancient banyan trees and a placid lake in the Canton suburbs. Here presides the Queen of Dim Sum, Madame Lau, whose genius is recognised by gourmets worldwide. It is quiet and tranquil compared with other *dim sum* restaurants and a treat to be remembered.

Shanghai

The cooking of Shanghai is a true melting pot. It would be much more accurate to label this gastronomic heritage Lower Yangzi Valley cooking. Shanghai was an insignificant hamlet before it was grabbed as a treaty port in 1841 so it has no traditional cuisine to call its own. Instead, it has borrowed widely from the surrounding rich delta areas, notably from the provincial kitchens of surrounding Jiangsu and Zhejiang provinces.

For a century, Shanghai was an international city and, despite 30 years of subjugation in the Maoist mould, there always remained a strong culinary influence from abroad. This was created by the once strong French presence in the city, by the hugh influx of White Russians and Jews who flocked there between the world wars, and by the big foreign populations of British, German, Danish, American and Japanese business communities. Stronger tasting, well oiled, cooked with more salt and copious quantities of sweet rice wine from the nearby city of Shaoxing, the food of the region is tasty and exciting.

Sichuan

A couple of thousand miles upriver from Shanghai is the Red Basin of Sichuan. The land gets its name from the deep maroon soil rather than the politics of its turbulent native sons; Deng Xiaoping and many other revolutionaries sprang from this red earth. Here is the peppery kingdom; the spicy, tangy dishes of Sichuan and nearby provinces of Hunan and Guizhou are renowned. Full of zest and

Famous author Lu Xun wrote many of his best-loved books, including 'The Story of Ah Q', in his home in Shaoxing. The house is preserved as a museum and the kitchen is that of a well equipped wealthy housewife in the 1920s.

colour, Sichuan dishes such as dried shredded beef and red peppers look as attractive as they taste.

Geography has played a major part in creating the Sichuan palate. Local gourmets tell you over a toast of *mao-tai* (which originated in Guizhou) that the intense humidity of summer causes hot flushes and bad tempers. The way to get rid of this troublesome complaint is to eat lots of hot, highly spiced foods. The chillies and peppers cause the blood temperature to rise, which opens the pores in the skin, which in turn allows the internal organs to cool off. Is there any truth in this old wives' tale? Who knows. Herbal doctors swear it's true and a lifetime addiction to hot red pepper didn't stop

Mao Zedong (from Hunan) living to a ripe old age. So, enjoy that sliced cold duck smoked in tea and camphor, sip the fragrant tea from the Sichuan hillsides where the pandas prowl at night and tuck into the chicken sautéed with red pepper. It may burn the roof off your mouth and bring tears to your eyes, but it's going to open the pores.

One curious footnote to Sichuan cuisine is the presence on the menu of seaweed. Here you have a place thousands of kilometres from the East China Sea and there is often seaweed on the table. Why? Once again, the explanation comes from the herbalists. More than 1000 years ago, the landlocked basin was noted for goitre. Many people suffered from the disease. Most of the local salt was obtained from bores where bamboo shafts were driven deep into the earth and a salt solution pumped laboriously to the surface.

Somehow, a herbal practitioner discovered the link between iodine salt in seaweed and goitre. Eat enough seaweed (they didn't know the specific chemical substance, of course) and goitre would gradually diminish. So up the Yangzi, struggling against the mighty flow of that phenomenal torrent, coolies have for centuries dragged big junkloads of seaweed to grace the tables of Sichuan's health-conscious gourmets.

Beijing

The cuisine of Beijing, like that of Shanghai, is a misnamed hybrid. It should more correctly be described as the culinary tradition of the North China Plain. Most dishes that are commonly thought of as Beijing food (including the famed Peking Duck) originated from fertile, food-loving Shandong province where Confucius 25 centuries ago presided over a rich mixture of philosophy and gastronomy. Within this realm of northern provinces where 'Beijing' food is the norm—roughly speaking, Shandong, Hebei, Shanxi, Shaanxi and the Manchurian lands—there is incredible culinary diversity. Some rules, however, apply to most of the area. Wheat buns and pancakes are the staff of life here, not rice. The food is solid, substantial peasant fare, aimed at keeping a man hard at work in the fields during those frigid northern winters.

Until the end of the 18th century, the vast expanse of Manchuria, ancestral homeland of the Qing Dynasty which had ruled China since 1644, was largely empty. The forests and grasslands were deemed an enormous reserve for the pleasure of the ruling nationality and Han Chinese were rigorously excluded and confined to a slice of land close to the southern coast of present-day Liaoning province. Then, as Manchu rule collapsed, Chinese poured into these empty lands. It was at the same time as the Americans rolled across the Mississippi and conquered the Wild West. The Chinese settlers headed into the empty Manchurian plains with much the same exhuberant enthusiasm as did the American settlers into the Great Plains. With them, they took their farming methods and culinary traditions. It explains why basic Shandong food serves as the strong foundations on which so much Northeast cooking skills are built today.

The Forgotten Four
There are many culinary schools in China outside the basic four.

Mongol
The Mongols, up on their harsh, windswept steppes, have their own traditions, adapted for the hard life of nomadic herders and roving invaders. Steak Tartare, that elegant dish served in western restaurants, can trace its beginnings to the armies of the Great Khan. As Genghiz and his extremely unfriendly horde galloped out of the steppes on their way to conquer the world, they rode fast and light. There was no large commissionary supply train rumbling in their wake. Instead, the rude, tough Mongols would cut a big chunk of meat off cattle, horse, sheep or goat and stick the raw, bleeding steak under their saddle. After a day of riding, the constant pounding

of the meat broke down the gristle and sinews and made it tender. They would tear into the slab of raw meat at the end of the day, toss down a leather flask of fermented horse milk and be up before dawn the following day to ride off to sack, plunder and rape another city.

Manchu

The Manchus were a little more civilised before they ascended the Dragon Throne. But not much. Their gastronomy was considerably elevated compared to that of the Mongols but nowhere near as civilised as the elegant Han they ruled. Lamb stews and beef barbecues were more their mark, along with heavy tubers and vegetables strong enough to last through the six-month-long icebox winters of their northern homeland.

Xinjiang

Much more exotic is the food of the far western lands of Xinjiang. The name means 'New Dominion' and signifies the late date at which it was reincorporated into the Chinese empire after centuries of uncertainty over who held sway over this vast, arid land. Islam came early here, and with Xinjiang bordering Central Asia and the population a majority of Turkic Uygurs and other non-Han races, one expects the food to be different. So it is. The caravanserais of Kashgar and Urumqi smack of herbs and spices of Araby. Camels wander the streets amid stands of hot charcoal over which Uygur chefs bake kebabs of lamb, peppers and onion on wooden stakes. (To many Chinese, particularly southerners, lamb has a distasteful odour and the smell of cheese frequently makes them nauseous. Here, lamb and cheese made from goat, horse and camel milk are much loved staples.)

Tibetan

The Tibetans, of course, have their own culinary culture which they seem to enjoy almost as fervently as their brand of Buddhism.

The best food in China is down on the farms with the people. If you are ever fortunate enough to be invited to join peasants in their homes, do so with alacrity. It is a great honour, marvellous fun and the best introduction you can get to the life of warm-hearted, wide-smiling Old Hundred Names. I had a wonderful time with the Wu family in the Yong River valley in Zhejiang.

The intricacies of both are likely to be lost on outsiders. Barley flour, known as *tsampa*, is the basis of just about everything, mostly because little other grain has ever been successful grown in the harsh climate on the high ice plateau. Ground barley is added to everything, from tea to minced beef to vegetables. It is the basis of all Tibetan food. Tea carried up from the lowlands of Sichuan is mixed with smelly yak butter and heavy handfuls of barley to make a staple drink; it tastes as bad as it sounds. There may well be some tasty Tibetan native dishes; if you ever find one, please tell me.

Every racial group, region and county in China has individual culinary traits which locals regard with strong native pride. To a Chinese, food is absolutely central to life, and pride in the heritage

187

of home village, county and province is supreme. Wherever you travel in China, always make sure to ask your guides, hotel staff and tour escorts what the local speciality is. Then try it.

Who knows, you might like it.

Manners Maketh Thee Hungry

When I first came to Asia in the early 1960s, my initial touch of the Chinese way of life came with a jolly band of newspapermen in an open-air cooked food stall in Singapore. Platter after steaming, aromatic platter arrived on the table. Chopsticks flashed like swords in a *kung fu* movie as those ravenous scribes attacked the chilli crab, steamed prawns and fish cooked with spring onions and ginger. Unaccustomed to the simple intricacies of the chopsticks, my pickings of the meal were slim indeed. Then a burly Singaporean of Hakka descent leaned over, drained his Tiger beer and explained the first rule of Chinese culinary etiquette. 'Always make sure you don't go hungry,' he advised. This has stood me in fine stead ever since.

The Restaurant

About the worst fate that can befall a serious diner is to find himself alone at a Chinese table. How can he or she sample more than two or three dishes? What a tragedy. The optimum number of people to enjoy a decent repast is a dozen. That's why Chinese dining tables are generously sized round affairs, so 12 hungry gourmands can gather around the rim and lean over to get at the dishes on the Lazy Susan in the middle that takes the dishes to within reach of all.

But if there are only two or three or four of you in a party, never mind. Just do your best and eat as much as you can. In many restaurants, the menu will list dishes in three sizes. If there are only a few of you, order the smallest size of every dish so you can call for as many different courses as possible.

The girth-conscious westerner can eat till he bursts with an easy conscience because the Chinese diet is the healthiest on earth.

The Table

Chinese eat as a family. That is why tables are so large. Based on the farming life, everyone could come in from the field and eat the steaming platters of vegetables and rice, along with the infrequent chicken, the festive piece of pork and the very rare bit of beef.

Chopsticks (*kuaizi*, or 'pick up small pieces') give longer reach. They are hygienic as well as efficient and well designed to allow deft diners to pluck tiny delicacies from stewpot or serving platter.

Etiquette

Table manners are as complex as they are simple. On the most basic level, tuck in and eat your fill. On more formal levels, the etiquette can be as disciplined as the court of Louis XVI.

Formal banquets can be fun, once in a while. But if you are doing serious business in China and are going to a banquet a night, you can soon weary of the endless courses of rich dishes.

Serving

The first platter at a banquet will be a spectacular selection of cold cuts and pickled vegetables. The host picks up a couple of choice items and places them on the plate of the guest of honour, then does the same for other guests within chopstick reach. Other members of the host party do the same. Then you have a toast—and tuck in.

Be careful. This is the first of a dozen dishes, so approach the meal like a marathon runner. This is no culinary hundred-metre dash. The waitress will display the courses so you can appreciate the appearance of the artistic creation (almost as important as taste) and then she will serve each diner. In less formal settings, the dishes will be put on the middle of the table and everyone helps themselves.

Timing

They eat early in China. The morning meetings end at 11.30 a.m. so everyone can scurry off to the dining table. At night, it's up chopsticks at 6 p.m. Until the tourist influx caused a change in habits, at least in the bigger hotels, meals were served from 6 p.m. and service stopped at 6.30 p.m. If you had not dined by then, well, tough. You had to wait till breakfast or munch a packet of dry biscuits in your hotel room.

As in so many other areas, there have been changes. Hotels now serve until 10 p.m. or so. But don't leave things too late or you might still go to bed hungry.

At a banquet, when the last course is served, usually fresh fruit, it is time to drink up and go. You don't sit around the dinner table for small talk. You've been at table for a couple of hours mixing conversation with the courses. Now you eat your orange or melon, raise your glass in a final toast, shake hands all round and repeat your sincere thanks for a marvellous meal—then depart. Chinese good manners call for a speedy end to conclusions once the final course is consumed.

Everything under the Sun

There's a saying: Chinese will eat any creature whose backbone points to the sun. In other words, any animal, fish or fowl is good for the pot. The hidden message here is that the only animal whose backbone does *not* point to the sun—man—is not eligible for the pot. This stricture has been relaxed among the Chinese communities of South America where upside-down sloths are sometimes a delicacy adapted to the Chinese kitchen.

In China, just about anything goes into the wok.

No Puss or Poodle

There is a story about eating in China that simply refuses to go away. Dozens of people will tell you they've heard of it second-hand. Nobody can ever give a time, date, place or name.

The story goes like this ...

An elegant foreign couple, normally identified as French, go

If it runs, walks, crawls, leaps, flies, waddles, hops, swims, glides or burrows, the Chinese will have a tried-and-tested recipe for it. This pangolin caught by tribesmen in Yunnan near the Vietnamese border made a prime dish. Serve it sautéed with a whisper of ginger and a hint of garlic and ginger, I was advised by a Yao chef. The recipe is simple: first, catch a pangolin ...

into a restaurant. Sometimes, the tale has them in Hongkong, other times in a city in China.

With them, the pair have a well-trimmed poodle on a leather lead. They cannot speak Chinese. A helpful waiter brings a menu. The couple cannot decipher a single character. The waiter points to what other diners are having. The couple look, nod.

The waiter kindly offers to take the dog outside while the couple dine. Thank you, monsieur.

In come the courses. Each, washed down by cold Qingtao beer, is tastier, more succulent, than the last. The couple dine excellently.

The bill is called for. So reasonable for such a feast! The couple pay, leaving a big tip.

Thank you, they say. Now, where is our pet? The waiter looks astonished. There is a communications gap. Finally, the message gets through. The dog? The waiter points proudly at one of the dishes in which the poodle has been tastily presented with garlic and ginger. The lady faints.

I've heard this story a score of times. Nobody has yet to persuade me it ever happened.

Munching on Monkey

Another great gastronomic horror story sworn to be true by hundreds of people who have never seen it is the old saga of eating the brains of a live monkey. This is usually said to take place in Borneo or Indonesia, but I've also heard tell of it being a practice in Guangxi or Yunnan provinces. It is a lot of nonsense but never let it be said I would ruin a good story just because it is not true.

The recipe for this imaginary feast is to take a live monkey. The circular table has a round hole about five inches in diameter cut in the middle. You (somehow) sit the monkey on a stool and strap it in place so the skull protrudes through the hole. Then, using a sharp knife, you cut off the top of the head and pick at the live brain.

This is total garbage, of course, but thousands of people who have never seen it swear it is true.

The old European ethnocentric fears about dining on dog or enjoying a well-sautéed cat steak in a Chinese restaurant is sheer nonsense. Old China Hands love to repeat such ridiculous yarns to turn the tender stomachs of the delicate newcomers.

Fear not. There is no way in the world anyone will be served dog instead of beef in a Chinese restaurant anywhere on earth. One reason this is unlikely is simple economics.

Chinese, especially in the south, do eat dogs in winter. But they are normally the plump Zhou puppies with black tongues, specially bred for the stew pot. Restaurants are not going to feed this delicacy to ignorant foreigners, if only because Zhou flesh costs about 15 times more than prime beef. It is eaten for medicinal purposes (it is supposed to make the blood thick and protect the elderly against winter chills) and is very difficult to find.

Nobody is going to waste this on a foreign devil who wouldn't appreciate such a fine dish.

Delicacies

That's not to say the Chinese don't have some peculiar tastes. If you should have a hankering after stirfried scorpions, hasten up to the western region of Shandong province and all your wishes will be answered. The poisonous creatures up there are a much adored speciality.

Truth to tell, they don't taste too bad. Every peasant farm seemingly has its own backyard scorpion plot; do not ask me how one breeds them. Whenever honoured guests appear on the horizon, Mrs Tsang goes outside and scoops up a couple of hundred 5 cm long scorpions. As any Shandong housewife will happily tell you, they have to be cleansed thoroughly twice in dry salt, then washed in salty water, to remove the venom in the tail. Then stirfried, they end up a crunchy delicacy tasting not unlike English whitebait. They are, I must admit, an acquired taste.

Rice birds? In the great southern ricelands, young sparrows 3 cm or so long are trapped as they flutter around the ripening crop. Marinated and then baked, they are eaten bones and all.

Snakes? You name it, Chinese eat it. Cobras are big favourites in Guangdong while pythons are the choice delight in Fujian. The true delicacy is the gall bladder. To the table, the waiter (brave fellow) brings a writhing 3-metre black king cobra. On his finger, the waiter wears a ring with a sharp hooked blade. He loops the hissing snake over the table, flashes his wrist and the gall bladder pops out of the snake and, twisting and oozing greenish bile, it sinks to the bottom of the glass of snake vodka in front of you. Being the only foreigner and therefore the guest of honour, you have won the great distinction of getting the gall bladder. There is no way you can get out of this. Lift your glass in a polite toast to the host and swirl down the contents with a satisfied smile. The first dozen times are the worst.

Bear's paws? These taste rather like rich oxtail stew. Pretty good. Now the central government has declared bears a protected species so this is a rare dish.

Camel hooves? Because it is now largely impossible for chefs to get bear's feet, they make do with camels. The awkward beasts plod by the millions over the steppes of Mongolia and the sands of Xinjiang so they are in no way an endangered species. Bad luck. This means there are an endless supply of camel's hooves to go around. A well-simmered, marinated camel's foot, boiled for hours with herbs and vegetables by a master chef and served with great flair and style, tastes just like what it is—the well-worn hoof of a critter than has walked through every sewer between Ulan Bator and Kashgar. Humps, another northern delicacy, are a delight compared to the hooves.

Pandas? No way. Anyone killing a panda for the pot in China faces life imprisonment.

Sea slugs. The only dish I flatly refuse to touch is this vile creature that oozes itself over shallow seas off the China coast. They are a prized delicacy. Imagine a truck tyre that had been on a vehicle used for 40 years or so to run about a farmyard. Cut off a chunk of tyre, throw it on a plate and you get some idea of what a good piece of sea slug tastes like.

Beancurd. Marvellous. Wonderful. The staff of life. The pressed whey of beans, usually soy, is one of the most healthy and joyous inventions of the Chinese kitchen. Alas, many westerners do not like the texture of *tofu* although doctors will tell you this protein-rich vegetable cuts cholesterol, replaces meat and has vast dietary advantages. Bland in itself, *tofu* can be mixed with a vast variety of other ingredients to give it a huge array of tastes. Thankfully, this marvellous dietary invention is now becoming popular among sophisticated western foodies.

Years ago, in the Hunan capital of Changsha, I was dining with a bunch of top party officials in a restaurant which Mao Zedong was said to have frequented when he was a young teacher in the town. How about a dish of the *tofu* which was the late Chairman's favoured dish, I suggested. This is a preparation called, with extremely good reason, Bad Smell Beancurd. There was some hesitation but the waiter was called and the dish eventually appeared. Never has a culinary invention been so aptly named.

It lay on the plate looking like something that had been deposited in a paddy field by a very sick water buffalo. It smelled bad, it looked bad and it tasted a lot worse. I took a hesitant mouthful with my chopsticks. Eyes turned in my direction. I swallowed, reached for a glass of the local firewater. The party secretary, mayor, propaganda chief and assorted officials looked anxiously on. My verdict? Well, I said, if this is the sort of stuff that Chairman Mao used to have to eat, then I was not surprised that he set off on the Long March.

Silence while this was translated. Then roars of laughter all round and calls for more rice wine and beer as the Bad Smell Beancurd was, thankfully, carried away to oblivion.

Exotica

Softshell turtles steamed in their shells with herbs, peppers and spices are a speciality of Guangxi. Zhuang tribesmen swear by the dish as a protection against the chills of winter. They hint also of the vast potential aid in the sexual department which a steady diet of stewed turtle provides.

A few years ago, the famed Cajun chef, John Folse of Louisiana, was in Hongkong cooking at the Hilton Hotel. One of his specialities from the Louisiana bayous was turtle. Astonishing. The dish tasted precisely as it was prepared in Guangxi. In some excitement, I talked to the chef after lunch. The recipe he gave me was exactly the same—the ingredients and the preparation—as that used in the hill valleys of southwest China. Come to think about it, we agreed after a lengthy discussion, why not? Both Louisiana and Guangxi are inhabited by people who are a minority (Cajun and Zhuang) and live in hot, humid areas, richly watered, well jungled where game and wildlife abounds. So it really shouldn't be too much of a surprise that the dishes were based on the same animals and vegetation and

cooked in the same manner. The moral of this story is that no matter how strange a dish may sound, it's well worth trying. It could be something just like mother cooked back home.

There are exceptions. I doubt if anyone's mother ever cooked fat frog soup, unless she was a Liaoning herbalist's mum. The winters in Manchuria are ferociously cold. Many animals, including the humble frogs, hibernate. In the autumn, a special breed of frog eats furiously, then burrows down into the fields and streambanks to create a warm environment for the coming deep freeze. The creatures are protected not only by their burrows but by rich, deep layers of fatty tissue built up during their summer-long feast. When the snows fall and the earth freezes solid, Manchurian gourmets set off in search of the buried frogs. They know how to find the animals in their deep hollows; don't ask me how. Once caught, the sleepy frogs are skinned and the layer of fat scraped off their hides. The fat is

197

boiled and made into a soup which supposedly does for the human diner what the fat was originally supposed to do for the frog. It keeps him warm in the plunging temperatures.

Worry not. No Chinese restaurant or hotel is going to press such delicacies on a squeamish westerner. But such potions, part food, part medicine, are common on the kitchen tables of China. They are the extreme equivalent of the Jewish mum's chicken soup. Most Chinese grandmothers, however, use duck as the raw ingredient.

A Diet of Desperation

Ever seen a shark's fin? They are ragged pieces of gristle and skin. There is not much taste to them and not a great deal of nutrition. So why are they now so vastly expensive and how come shark's fin soup is a renowned delicacy?

The questions hark back to the days of famine along the coast. Why eat a fin if large chunks of succulent shark flesh were available? Simply because there was not enough food to go around and if the fin was all that was left to boil up to keep alive, people would eat it. Probably by accident, someone discovered that the fin, boiled sufficiently long, produced a strong gelatinous substance. In time, this was added to chicken broth to produce the tasty, rich dish known today as shark's fin soup. Originally, however, it was eaten because there was nothing else. It was part of the diet of desperation that led Chinese over the centuries to place many items of exotica on the table.

Buying Food

The shops of China are bursting. Unlike the pitiable display of foodstuffs available in the Soviet bloc, China luxuriates in plentiful supplies of the basic necessities of life. Cooking oil and grain sold under controlled prices are sometimes rationed but there is always plenty available at slightly higher prices in the free enterprise markets.

Shops and outside markets are normally bustling. This is partly because of the traditional insistence on the freshest possible ingredients (fish are scooped live from holding tanks, chickens beheaded and plucked in front of you) which sees housewives going to market every morning. This desire for fresh food is compounded by necessity; not every home in China has a refrigerator and daily buying is vital.

The shopping visit is partly recreational. It's an opportunity to talk to the neighbours, see friends, stop for a chat and find out what's going on in the neighbourhood. You don't only load up on spinach and carp, you also collect the daily ration of gossip.

For foreigners, western-style delicatessens now offer well stocked premises, usually in joint venture hotels. But people who live in China will probably buy most of the basic vegetables, poultry, fish and canned foods from local markets. For one thing, it's a lot cheaper. For another, it's more fun.

Don't Just Eat Food, Talk About It

Just about every Chinese considers himself an expert on food. It is a universal fascination. Sophisticated cosmopolitans and simple peasants alike are happy to discuss food, knowledgeably and with great enthusiasm, with just about anyone. If the novice businessman in China wants to swiftly gain friends and influence people, he would be well advised to bone up on Chinese cuisine so he can make intelligent table talk. (Chinese consider it polite to talk about food and to ignore more controversial matters like religion, politics and money.)

I was once at a high-level political seminar at the Great Hall of the People in Beijing. There were senior cadres there from every province and a collection of top party and government officials. Up to me came a member of the State Council who quietly took me aside for a chat. The other foreign newspapermen were, understandably, anxious to know what we had discussed so earnestly in the 15 minutes we were chatting animatedly in a corner.

'Matters of mutual interest,' I announced, copying a line much loved by diplomats. This, of course, infuriated my colleagues. They thought I'd got a scoop. Alas, no. What the Great Man wanted was to talk to me about a recipe in one of my recently published Chinese cookbooks. The ingredients were a bit different in my directions from the way the dish was prepared in his home province. We spent a lively time swapping anecdotes about smoked duck (every region has a distinctive method of preparing this delicious dish) and sundry other dishes. I didn't get a story that night but it did me absolutely no harm at all to have been seen cornered with one of the most powerful men in the land at a public function. In months to come, down in the provinces, when I saw local leaders who had been at this reception, I got an overwhelming welcome. It took some time for my western colleagues to get over their ire. When I eventually told them later that night we had discussed cookbooks and recipes, they flatly refused to believe me.

But it is the mark of a scholar, gentleman and sophisticate to be able to knowingly talk about *haute cuisine*. The kitchen door opens many other doors in China.

Chapter Ten

THE FAMILY

With perfect harmony in the family
No evil influences can injure

Everything prospers in a united family
Though events do not happen according to men's calculations

The extended family is the basis of Chinese life and society. It is an institution that has prevailed throughout the ages. It remains inviolate today, the foundation of Chinese culture and community.

The family was the obvious first organisation to exist when cave age men started scratching the fertile earth in the Great Bend of the Yellow River to grow their meagre crops. The very first ruler of an early Chinese state, the great Hao Fuh Hi, is reputed to have formulated the extended family clan system and to have laid down rules for the use of family names sometime about 2850 BC. Through all the agonies and triumphs of Chinese history since then, the family has remained the strongest strand running through civilisation.

The Wong Family

The family today is Mr Wong, Mrs Wong and one little Wong. There is a generation growing up which largely will never know the dubious joy of having a brother or sister. The stringent restriction on children may be for the good of the nation but it cuts across the ingrained attitudes of thousands of years.

Going Home

The casual tourist to China today is unlikely to visit a Chinese family in their home. This is especially so in the cities where accommodation is in very short supply. Many people live in such crowded conditions that to the westerner would be intolerable.

So don't expect to be invited home by some casual acquaintance. Through television and movies, most Chinese you meet, especially if they speak a foreign language, are fully aware of the chasm between their homes and what foreigners enjoy. They are hesitant to ask foreigners home, even if they feel like it, because of mutual embarrassment when a visitor is ushered into a flat the size of a modest bedroom in a western home.

If an opportunity should arise, grab it. They don't happen often.

The average home in a city is likely to be in a concrete block no more than five storeys high. These are the new uniform buildings thrown up the length of China to accommodate the mushrooming urban population. Housing the 200 million people now crammed into the cities is a vast headache for central planners who have called on international urban experts for advice on how to house people in liveable conditions.

You are much more likely to be asked to enter a home when you are strolling through some village a bit off the beaten track. If this should happen, nod your thanks and go inside.

Generally homes in the southern hamlets are larger than in the north. There are two reasons for this, both basic. The south is richer, therefore they can build more spacious homes. In the north, homes have to be heated for six frigid months of the year so the snugger the better.

When you are ushered into a Chinese home, city or country, it will appear to you to be spartan beyond belief. Pride of place will probably be given to a television set and radio. There will be pictures of relatives and ancestors mounted on the main wall. Take one of the chairs offered, sip your tea and say 'Xie xie ni'. Your politeness will be appreciated.

When exchanging, through your interpreter, details of where you come from and what you do, glance around. To your eyes, the situation may appear grim. But the householder is obviously proud to show off her home. Why? Because for her, a decade ago such luxuries as you see would have been unthinkable. It is the economic revolution of Deng Xiaoping that has made it possible. So admire what you see, ask for details about the family pictures and think only to yourself how far the Chinese people have yet to go to achieve a better standard of living.

Family Planning

Since the 1970s, China has been desperately trying to bring down the soaring rate at which the population had been climbing. The reason was survival; projections showed that if nothing was done to check the rising population, China would by 1989 have had 1.3 billion people. As it was, members of the Family Planning Commission in Beijing could report there were 1.127 billion in

April of that year. With an extra 200 million mouths to feed—
'avoided births' as officials put it—much of the economic progress
made in recent years would have been nullified.

When Mao Zedong proclaimed the People's Republic in 1949,
there were 540 million people in China. By the trends that became
apparent in the early 1970s, the population by the turn of the century
would have reached 1.5 billion, a staggering burden to support.
Even with the stringent family planning programmes introduced by
worried officials in 1972, China will still have 1.2 billion citizens
when the nation enters the 21st century.

Why? One direct reason is better health care. By western
standards, the hospitals in rural China may be primitive. But the
Barefoot Doctors scheme introduced in the 1950s had hardy volunteer
paramedics tramping through every village in the land preaching
simple lessons of hygiene, basic first aid, ground rules in caring for
newborn babies. China didn't have much money, drugs or modern
facilities and in that hostile era there was no foreign aid but the
message got through. It helped keep alive millions of babies who
otherwise would have died. So did vaccinations that saved millions
from diseases like polio, measles and smallpox.

With fewer people dying and more being born, the population
soared.

One-child Families

In 1979, officials ruled that married couples should not be permitted
to have more than one child. 'One is enough,' proclaimed posters
that went up all over the land. With 150,000 doctors, counsellors
and advisers on the staff and with another 300,000 auxiliary staff
stationed throughout the country, the Family Planning Commission
spread the message enthusiastically.

Those who followed the strictures were rewarded with housing,
job promotion, choice perks and public acclaim. Those who
determinedly kept breeding lost out on financial bonuses, were

publicly scorned, had job opportunities blocked and in extreme cases were sacked; if they were members, they were expelled from the Communist Party.

The twin carrot and stick approach worked. The birthrate dropped, but not sufficiently. Still, the economic impact was considerable. The education campaign, abortions, the supply of free birth control pills, condoms and other scientific aids and financial inducements—plus the patriotic urging to help the nation by making the sacrifice of having only one child—meant there were 200 million fewer people born than would otherwise have been the case.

Traditionally, much of the wealth of the peasants had been measured in the number of children they had. There were many reasons for this. The major two were the necessity for a son to carry on the proud family name and to provide children to worship the ancestors. The other was to ensure that in old age, an infirm peasant would have an ample supply of filial sons to support him.

Attempting to change the inherited habits and inbuilt mores of thousands of years was no easy matter. Particularly in rural areas, there was great opposition. Horrifying stories emerged from rural areas, backed by official statistics, about girl babies being killed or simply left to die so parents could try again for the prized boy baby needed to carry on the family line.

To counter this, the policy was relaxed. If a couple had a girl, they could try again, after a waiting period of a few years, to produce a boy.

The Super Brats

Some cynics say the one-child household has produced a breed of brats. They contend that with only one baby on which to expend their love, parents spoil solo children, and that doting grandparents add even more to the problem.

Others argue that children cannot have too much love. Certainly, the new generation of China could be called with some justification The Prized Generation. They are bigger, heavier and brighter than children born 40 years ago. A special institute at Hangzhou University has been established to track the physical growth and mental development of the nation's youngsters. Statistics show children today are healthier, livelier and have a higher IQ than in their grandparents' time.

Any visitor to China can see the results of one-child families. The children are well dressed, well loved, well clothed, well fed, well educated. Because parents know they can only have one of them, they strive to give their children the best.

The spoilt generation? I think not. The lucky generation is more like it. Anyone who has travelled in other Asian lands and seen the child beggars starving in the streets and then observed the happy, adored children of modern China has no doubt of the success of the one-child, one-family policy.

Family Structure

The structure of the Chinese family was well in place before Confucius set down the guidelines that have endured for 2500 years. Traditional social values emphasising respect for the elders and reverence for the ancestors are still a living part of Chinese daily life. In every humble peasant cottage to which I have been invited over the years, the main room is dominated by a montage of photographs and portraits and a shrine which contains incense.

The family is not just dad, mum and the kids as in the western world.

The extended family (*jia ting*) probably all live under one roof. This is how the first peasant families grouped before the dawn of history. A man and his wife and their children and grandchildren would live in one building. The man was the patriarch whose whim was law.

In modern China today and in the great Overseas Chinese

communities abroad, parents are respected and deferred to in a degree that foreigners find incomprehensible. A successful middle-aged businessman or bureaucrat will still pay formal respect to his humble peasant parents and unabashedly follow their wishes.

Relationships

Confucius laid down precepts for how people should relate to each other. The basic ones are:

1. Between husband and wife
2. Between parents and children
3. Between brothers and sisters
4. Between sovereign and subjects
5. Between friends

There is also a special relationship between students and teachers, one that does not end with graduation but which extends throughout a lifetime. This is similar to the bonds between parents and children; what the father does in the home, the teacher continues in the classroom.

Old Age

The venerable old man is a familiar and much loved part of Chinese literature and painting. 'A man of 70 is a rarity from the ancient times' proclaims a proverb from the Tang Dynasty. True; life expectancy in those days was such that few reached their three score years and ten.

The elderly were—and are still—granted reverence not because they are rarities today in an era when Chinese longevity produces many millions of septuagenarians, but largely due to the deep experience in life and wisdom they are felt to have garnered over a lifetime.

When a man or woman completes the cycle of the 60-year calendar (time for the party of a lifetime and a banquet at which every family member will make enormous sacrifices to be present) he or she reaches a social plateau. With every year that passes, they acquire more dignity and status.

In the old days, a man of 60 could carry a staff within his village. By the age of 70 he could walk with the aid of the staff—symbol of longevity—in the country, and by the age of 80, he could carry it before the Dragon Throne and did not have to kneel before the emperor. Anyone who reached the age of 90 was regarded as being sufficiently venerable for the emperor to heed his advice.

Instead of being sent away to institutions and old folks' homes to spend their last days, a concept that profoundly shocks most Chinese, the elderly are treasured. Sons and daughters feel it is an honour and a privilege to have their parents living with them, even in the confines of a crowded city apartment or a small village house.

Kinfolk

Unlike the normal western family of a couple and their children, the Chinese bonds extend much further. Unmarried daughters live with their parents. When they are married, they traditionally sever links with their own family and their names are added to the ancestral family tablets of the husband's clan. The newlywed bride then owes allegiance and obedience to her mother-in-law with whom she will probably live. (The tyrannical attitude of the imposing matriarch over the pretty wife of First Son is a common, popular and enduring theme in Chinese literature that can be traced back at least 3000 years.)

Sons were encouraged to live with their parents until the elders died. This may have been possible when families clustered together in a clan village as tillers of the soil. Obviously, this is quite unrealistic in a modern urban industrial community. The custom for the eldest son to stay with the parents, however, is still common. After all, he is responsible for paying homage to the ancestors and when his parents do go to join the generations that went before, First Born will take his prideful place as head of the family.

The extended family will make great efforts to gather for special occasions, notably the great annual celebration of Lunar New Year. This remains constant under the communist regime; at New Year holidays are given so millions can travel from one end of the country to the other. To screen suspicion that this is based on 'ancient superstition', the occasion is officially the 'spring festival'.

Family Trees

Chinese genealogists can trace back the history of notable families for many generations. Wealthy and scholarly families proudly display the well thumbed, hand-bound books of characters that form their family trees. For peasant families, there is no such need for paper proof of their forebears; they have tilled the land around the village for centuries and the names are recorded in the hamlet temple.

The system is highly structured. Not only does it extend upwards and backwards, but also sideways. Second Aunty's Third Daughter is a close relative. Fourth Uncle's First Born is a close cousin, much more so than in the west. The relation of an individual to the rest of the clan extends outwards in a pattern similar to a boulder thrown into a goldfish pond. The most distant ripple may be far away, but it is still connected to the original splash of impact; so is a fourth cousin on the mother's side of the family still a relative and a person to be considered before any outsider.

The complex pattern of kinship is like a spider's web. Everyone is connected. In some charts that lay out an extended family, the person who is paying a genealogist to have his family mapped out will appear in the centre. Above him are his ancestors, below his descendants, children and grandchildren. To the right are his male relatives, to the left his father's female ancestors.

The Family Name

Taking precedence over all other consideration is the sacred family name and the filial duty of preserving it and passing it on to another generation. Hence the intense pressure to produce sons. If the eldest son has no son himself, tradition rules he must adopt the eldest son of his next youngest brother. If this cannot be done, the search goes on, spreading through the kinship network of male cousins.

If no acceptable candidates can be found within the clan, the search for an adoptive son can go outside, preferably to a sister's child. The sister, of course, is technically now a member of another family. The last alternative to keep alive the family name is for the husband of a daughter to be invited to join the father-in-law's family; their sons will bear the ancestral clan name and through this stratagem the honoured surname will live on and the ancestors will be worshipped for further generations.

Close Bonds

Relationships of all kinds are far more important to Chinese than to westerners. The intense bonds of the nuclear family can be grasped more easily by foreigners. But there are links of surprising closeness and strength between more distant relatives and friends.

These bonds extend to classmates in middle school, the western equivalent to high school. Decades after they have graduated, businessmen who went to an obscure high school will gather at old boys' nights. College alumni have similar feelings of affection and gratitude to their alma mater to a much more intense degree than Europeans or Americans.

Close associations are also found within professional and trade groups where affiliations are strong. This Chinese feeling of togetherness, of close association with people of the same background and similar interests, extends to all walks of life.

Birth

Some traditions surrounding pregnancy and birth date back to pre-history. Praying for a son is one of them. Modern Chinese will sometimes say they don't care if their sole baby is a boy or girl; one suspects the yearning for a male heir to carry on the family name is as ardent in the heart of a sophisticated city cadre as it is in a peasant in a rural hamlet.

Despite great advances in medicine which were aimed specifically at lowering the appalling death rate among babies in pre-revolutionary times, old superstitions die hard. Old wives' tales often linger on in the field of midwifery. Babies were traditionally not bathed for three days. Relatives were invited on the third day to view the newest family member.

If the baby survives a month, the official celebration is held when friends and acquaintances join in the fun. At First Moon parties, drinks and food are served. The male child's hair was once shaved off on the 29th day of life and wrapped in red cloth which was sewn into the baby's bedclothes. One hundred days later, the hair was thrown into a lake or river. This was meant to ensure the boy grew up brave and strong. This and other old superstitions are not practised these days—or are not admitted to.

Marriage

The institution of marriage was ordained by the very first known ruler of China, the great Hao Fuh Hi, in 2852 BC. Rites for wedlock were laid down in recognisable forms by the Duke of Zhou 3000 years ago and were carried out in that style until the end of the Qing Dynasty in 1911. Some elements of these old customs are still used today.

In the age of matchmakers, the old crone representing the man's family would approach the woman's clan. Token presents (a symbolic plump goose was favoured) were given, horoscopes exchanged. If the offer was not wholly unacceptable, the girl's details would be written on red paper and given to the matchmaker who would return to the man's family.

After a professional seer had scanned the horoscopes and all parties were satisfied, red cards with the family background of the pair were exchanged. This signified a betrothal. The potential bride and groom at this stage were not consulted.

Then presents were exchanged between the families and yet another professional was paid to find an auspicious date. Finally, the groom, relatives and friends went to the girl's home and accompanied her to his home, where she would then become part of his family. In olden times, this was often the first occasion the two most concerned with the procedure had met.

The young Republic of China passed laws simplifying these ancient procedures. In the first year of its rule, the communist regime passed the new marriage law that made free choice of partners the basis for wedlock, gave women equal rights and legal protection.

Wedding Parties

The customary puritanism of the new regime banned traditional expensive frills like wedding parties. In the past decade, there has been a reversion to lavish nuptial celebrations. These have been roundly criticised in the official press although some of the most expensive banquets of recent times have been held to mark the weddings of the offspring of senior cadres.

The newly prosperous business elite are returning to the old days with a vengeance. The father's family foots the bill for huge banquets in the best restaurant in the city and traditional robes are worn.

Divorce

Before reform laws this century, divorce was relatively easy. If you were a man. Should you have been a woman, divorce was impossible.

Customary laws under dynasties stretching for thousands of years allowed men to unload their spouses for trivial failings. These included:
1. Inability to bear a male child
2. Wanton conduct

3. Being disrespectful to her parents-in-law
4. Being talkative
5. Theft
6. Jealousy
7. Having an incurable disease

Jealousy could include a wife's reluctance to accept her husband taking in concubines. This was a common custom before the communist takeover. In theory, Confucian preachings held that a man could take a concubine if his wife was infertile or bore only daughters. In practice, a man could pack his home with as many women as he could support. The wife was supposed to be a devoted and dutiful spouse and to grin and bear it. The positive side of the argument was that if any of the concubines had children, they officially became the offspring of the Number One wife.

In theory and practice today, divorce is comparatively easy for Chinese, both men and women. In reality, the rate of marriage collapses is rare.

Dying

If you see people shrouded in white with their heads bound in similar material, you are watching a family grieve for a loved one. White is the colour of mourning in China.

Just as modern China has tried to eliminate or reduce the extravagances of marriage ceremonies, so have efforts been made to cut down the costs of funerals. In legend and literature, stories of families going into debt to pay for a fitting farewell to a patriarch are familiar. The genteel poor once saved half their lifetimes to pay for a decent funeral. The poor joined funeral societies in which they pooled their money to ensure that all members were sent off to the uncertainties of the next life in a fitting fashion.

This meant to be well clothed, buried in a coffin carved from good wood (if possible, wood from the Nan tree that grows in Sihuan) and laid to rest in a plot of ground guaranteed not to disturb the many deities of the Chinese heavens.

With the deep belief in ancestor worship and the twice yearly pilgrimage to family graves, this has in effect meant a great deal of land throughout the nation was being used as graveyards. Flying over China, you can see how hillsides around villages are pitted with gray spots. These are tombs of former generations.

Funerals

Once grandiose, the final ceremonies are now more spartan and confined to the family. But, as in so many other spheres, there has been considerable relaxation in recent years and ancient ceremonial trappings are making a reappearance.

These include the use of fiery offerings to the dead. If a man in life liked good food and drink, then cardboard and paper imitations of a feast may be burned at his funeral, reminders to the gods to cater for his needs in the afterlife. There are also wardrobes of paper clothes, paper boats, motorcars and, of course, huge wads of paper money printed by the Bank of Hades with minimum denominations of a million yuan to provide ample spending money in the next world.

Chapter Eleven

DOWN IN THE COUNTRY

When you drink water,
Think of the source.

The great cities may be the elegant, graceful stars in the Chinese cultural heaven. The heart, soul and belly of the land is the village. Here in the countryside is where the bulk of China lives. It is here that the pure 'Chineseness' of the people can be seen.

In many ways, the prodigious output of the Chinese farmer more resembles gardening than farming. Plots are very small by western standards; a family in the fertile south where classical rice paddy

Rice paddies, neat plots of vegetables and stone houses, the common conception of how the countryside should look often turns out to be reality as scenes like this appear out of the Hubei mist like a scene from a willow pattern plate.

farming is practised probably has less than two acres. Every inch of ground is used.

North of the Yangzi in the wheat and millet growing areas, agriculture is equally intense. The land is nurtured with nightsoil and commercial fertiliser. The ceaseless pattern of preparing the fields, fertilising the soil, planting seeds, weeding, raking, hoeing, reaping, harvesting is as set in the mores of Chinese rural life as the rising and setting of the sun.

In the south, with three crops a year, thanks to the warm, humid climate, the pattern is a bit different from the arid, cooker north where the frigid winters reduce crops to one a year. Everywhere, there is a pattern, a rhythm to life, that has been established down the ages. Around the confluence of the Wei River with the Huanghe, man has planted the same fields for at least 6000 years.

That good earth of China still supports the nation. The village is the foundation of Chinese culture. Old Hundred Names, the peasant, is the sturdy, patient, ancient stalwart who ultimately is the basis of the state, the nation and the race.

A Frenzy of Construction

At first, I didn't believe Madame Guo Xiao-lin. The Governor of Jiangsu, China's richest province, was trying to tell me that in the previous five years, more than half the 60 million peasants in Jiangsu had moved into new homes. Pure propaganda, I thought. Couldn't be done. Fifty per cent of the population in new houses in five years? No way. Over the next couple of weeks, I travelled hundreds of kilometres through the province. Looking out the train windows, directing my hire car drivers down lonely side roads to remote villages, peering from the decks of ships sliding down the Yangzi, I kept a count. Sure enough, China's top woman politician had been telling the truth. Staggering as it seemed, the claims were correct.

That was a few years ago and the building boom in rural China continues in a frenzy of construction. The sturdy houses being constructed in every province are spacious and comfortable buildings, superior in every way to the lamentable hovels which traditionally provided humble roofs over the head of the Chinese peasant. I am no propagandist for the communist system. But the visitor to China cannot escape the plain fact that the man-in-the-paddyfield is on the whole better housed today than at any time in the past 5000 years.

Housing differs in accordance with the climate. Everywhere, however, the new homes tend to be bigger, constructed of higher grade materials and offer superior accommodation. This frantic building boom has not been without its drawbacks. The demand for materials, notably cement, roofing tiles and timber, has caused shortages and has led to inflation. Much more seriously, the new-found peasant wealth, created by the economic policies that let them plant what they want and sell their produce, has created many problems.

The most obvious of these can be seen by anyone flying at low level over any part of densely populated, heavily tilled East China. For centuries, the villages have clustered amid the fields. The richest land was closest to the village. As new houses have gone up, they ringed the existing settlement, eating into the fields. The old homes in the centre of towns have often been turned into halls or commercial areas and as new larger homes have been built on the fringe, they have devoured some of the most productive agricultural land in China.

This situation is worrying economists and agronomists in Beijing. The statistics they produce show why; in the past decade, China has lost a staggering amount of prime cropland because of housing expansion—fields equal to the entire arable area of France have fallen out of agricultural use. When you consider that China's cultivable land is a mere 10 per cent or less of the total area, little wonder that central government planners become frantic about this effect of prosperity on future production.

The Greatest Achievement

Beijing can boast with considerable justification of the success of its agricultural policies. They manage what many considered impossible; they feed 1,127,000,000 people. There is no famine in China. Although there is some worry about lack of grain—largely because farmers prefer to grow more profitable crops of vegetable, cotton or even flowers—there is ample food to feed the enormous population. To many people, this victory is the greatest achievement of the Beijing government and goes a very long way towards balancing deficiencies in other areas. Is it better to have democracy or a full belly? Western idealists may have one answer. A starving Indian peasant in Bihar who has rights at the ballot box and a dying baby may well have an opposite opinion.

The Good Earth

Credit for the well-stocked markets of China does not belong merely to the central government. When the communists came to power, they had already 20 years experience in governing rural areas, first in the Soviet area of Jiangxi province, then in large areas of the north which they governed after the Long March. They had learned from earlier mistakes and realised that Soviet-style policies would not work in agriculture.

Still, the ardent revolutionaries attempted to tamper with Old Hundred Names and the way in which he tilled the good earth of China. They also tried to force a major change in lifestyle. First, peasants were encouraged to work in collectives. By 1958, the commune system was widely introduced; it merged large-scale agriculture with local government, public works and industry. This was the so-called Great Leap Forward which resulted in a Huge Plunge Backwards.

At the very least, three million people starved to death as a direct result of the Great Leap, one of the most disastrous economic policies ever attempted. In Guangdong and other areas, people in what had once been prosperous counties awash with rice were resorting to cannibalism to stay alive.

At the same time, experiments in communal living were suggested with children being taken away to special schools and adults sleeping in dormitories. This madness took two or three years to dissipate until even Mao Zedong was forced to admit the lunacies of his idealistic Brave New World policies.

For the peasants, these years were a living nightmare. The very foundations of rural life, the eternal Chinese family structure, was threatened. In the countryside, the Cultural Revolution of the next

219

Harvesting sugar in Guangxi; women are a vital part of the rural workforce.

decade went largely unnoticed. It was the Great Leap debacle that devastated rural China.

The political policies that shackled China's farmers were lifted in 1978 when the central government announced new rules. Put simply, these meant the people-on-the-land could by and large grow what they wished and sell it to whom they wanted for the best price they could obtain. Simple enough, you might think. But in the Chinese context they were revolutionary moves. They let the peasant get on with what he knew best, growing crops and raising livestock, and removed the nonsensical political burdens. The result was swift —farm income rose dramatically.

Prosperity Strides the Land

The results of this soaring income are obvious. First, there are those new homes. Wander into any Chinese village, find the centre of

Across a flooded paddy field, a peasant follows his water buffalo. It could be anywhere south of the Yangzi but this was in Hainan Island, China's 'Hawaii'.

town and sit down at a stall or restaurant. At first, if you are in a small place away from normal tourist haunts, the people may be reserved. Chances are, they are shy. Smile, and you'll reap a rich harvest of beams. Try out your patchy Putonghua. You'll soon be the centre of a crowd of curious folk. Give out cards (make sure you've printed a couple of thousand) that give not only your name, but your home town and country. Almost certainly, you'll soon be invited into a nearby home. In the cities, such an invitation is rare. Down in the countryside, the doors are flung open. All over the land, I've noticed the same warm greeting.

The inquisitive visitor who wants to see how national policies are affecting the normal people can stroll away by himself down some back lane, wandering through the narrow lanes just wide enough for a water buffalo or a donkey cart. Peer into the courtyards where much of family life is concentrated. The sight of a foreign

Two curious youngsters come up to say hello to a tourist.

face will soon have the kids coming out, then the grandparents. '*Ni hao*,' and waved invitations beckon you into the courtyard. Hands are shaken. You are gestured and bowed inside.

By the standards of the western world, the room may seem a poor enough place. Viewed through Chinese eyes, it is a treasury of prized possessions. The main room is probably about 5 by 3 metres. It is dominated by the inevitable TV set which, if China Central

Television is on the air, is turned on although nobody is watching.

On the wall, above a small shrine, are family photographs. In many homes, the patriarch will be pictured as a young man in military uniform, particularly if he was in the Peasants and Workers Red Army before Liberation. In a surprising number of homes, a portrait of Chairman Mao will be clustered with the family pictures. (I have never seen a portrait of Comrade Deng in a family collection.) On your unexpected impromptu visit, you will notice many signs of prosperity. Out in the yard, there are likely to be a couple of bicycles. Costing about three months' pay for the average factory worker, these are sizeable investments. Inside, the main room will have a bed because it is probably here that the main husband and wife in the household live. Other beds, usually foldable, are stacked in small rooms alongside. Cooking is usually done over coal stoves in a separate annex across the courtyard.

Under the family portraits, there will be a radio. A sewing machine may stand in a corner. If you are polite, you will express curiosity about the home. Chinese are unabashed askers of personal and financial questions. How long have you lived here? Where did you live before? How much did the television cost? Do you get the coal issued free (as happens in some of the coal-rich northern provinces) and if not how much do you pay every year? How much does rice cost a kilo? What about cooking oil? What do you grow? How much do you get for your crop? Who do you sell it to? How much does fertiliser cost? Where does the rest of your family work?

In turn, the peasants will want to ask you similar questions about your life back home in the Midwest or Midlands. I usually take a few dozen small coins with me when I go to China. It would be insulting to offer money to your sudden hosts who will press hot tea on you and offer you food. But if you offer a Hongkong $1 coin (worth about US15 cents) to a child, pointing out the head of Queen Elizabeth II, the family will be delighted with such an exotic talking point. (This, however, can lead you into deep political discussions;

what had the English monarch got to do with a Chinese city like Hongkong?)

Voluble, humorous, lively, inquisitive, shy and hesitant at first, but then open and friendly, the Chinese peasant at home is a relaxed and cheerful host.

Life Down on the Farm

Just as the lure of bright city lights dragged generations of European and American youths from the farms into the towns, so did similar urges work in China. The new prosperity in the countryside seems to have at least partially stopped this trend.

The best wage a young factory worker can expect is about 150 yuan a month. Then he has to pay for food and lodging. If he stays down on the farm, he is likely these days to do a lot better. Farm income is soaring.

Families that live close to major cities can easily earn up to RMB10,000 a year. The main source of income is fresh vegetables and fruit which are taken to city or suburban free markets for daily sale. The profits, incredible for China, have fuelled a buying spree in the countryside.

The age-old sight of a water buffalo plodding through a muddy field in front of a farmer is now rare. These days, the peasant is more likely to be driving a small tractor which is made in factories in almost every province. (Interestingly, the tractors differ from place to place, with designs adapted to various climatic and typographical conditions. Most can also be swiftly converted from ploughing machines to small trucks to carry the harvest to market.)

Crafts

Traditionally, the Chinese peasant made just about everything he needed. Or, to be a lot more accurate, she did. Wives and daughters spent much time around the home weaving, making rattan furniture and creating household goods like wooden buckets. These days, the old folk crafts are largely disappearing, another victim of prosperity. Why spend many long hours laboriously making a watertight bucket out of wood when a plastic bucket that will last for eternity can be bought for a couple of yuan at the nearby market town?

The more basic crafts and arts have long been a feature of village life. Although the elegant arts were confined to the cities and the courts, the daily crafts were always practised in the villages and towns. They are still flowering today.

In many small villages, there are traditions of pottery and weaving rattan. In some tribal areas, vivid local arts, drawings, sophisticated carvings and beautiful pottery can be found for sale at very cheap prices. You've got to be lucky.

My tip is for you to wander about any marketplace you spot. Chances are the only thing you get will be photographs of squirming tanks of snakes or a wandering herbalist making his potions from stomach-queasy ingredients. On the other hand, you may find some local artist who is selling his pots or local crafts that intrigue or attract you. I like buying some of the exotically shaped steamers and pots used by peasants for winter hot-pot cooking. Not only are they very functional, they are also things of simple beauty. Teapots are another fascination for me and I snap up pots of all shapes and sizes to add to my collection. You never know what you are going to spot in country markets. It's always worth the effort to wander around and have a look.

Fun

Just as western culture has its harvest festivals, so do the peasants of China celebrate bringing in the crops. Travelling through the country in the autumn (the weather is better then, too), the visitor is likely to see crowds gathering in the streets. Sometimes, large temporary sheds will be thrown up or outdoor stages erected. Contortionists, acrobats, singers, opera shows and all sorts of open-air entertainment take place.

225

Wander in. If there is a charge, someone will show you how much to pay. It will be very cheap. This is how the people of China entertained themselves for centuries when troupes of minstrels, thespians and singers wandered the country, bringing lively artistic shows to the most remote areas. Television has killed much of this tradition (just as the music hall died in the western world) but some traces remain.

In rural areas, always ask your guides or at hotels what local festivals are being held. There's not going to be a great deal else to do, so wander down to the town square or marketplace and see how the rural folk of China enjoy themselves. In remote areas, you'll probably find yourself the star attraction.

— *Chapter Twelve* —

TIPS FOR SURVIVAL

Seeing once is better than hearing a hundred times.

Most foreigners who go to China do so as tourists. Their stays are going to be for less than a month. No matter how strange a new society is, it can be borne for a few weeks even if the food is weird, the language totally incomprehensible and the daily habits and customs of the inhabitants are sufficiently bizarre as to be matters of constant wonder.

It's different for those whose job or academic path takes them to a new society for a much longer period. They have to learn to make adjustments to fit in with their new environment. China is not going to change to suit them. If they want to survive, they have to adapt to their temporary homeland. This is now a lot easier to do than it was several years ago. But there are still considerable difficulties.

Your Family

You think it's tough being a businessman in China? You've got it easy, pal. Every day, your mind is occupied with problems, you have the stimulation of meeting new people, seeing fresh faces, gaining extra insights into the society with which you must now cope. Things are much tougher for the wives left to spend the day in an apartment or, even worse, in the confines of a hotel room.

They are even more stifling for the children. Imagine yourself a western teenager in China. Back home, life would be an endless round of school, parties, picnics, sports events, fashions, dating, overnight stays with friends, trips to the countryside, movie-going, hobbies and all the other joys of growing up and exploring life. In China, life is much more restricted. There are far fewer opportunities for enjoying the best years of your life.

Western children in China are well aware of how they are being deprived of what they see as the fun and glamour of life back in Los Angeles, Munich or Nottingham. And they are not grateful to their parents for dragging them off to live in a country where teenage jollity is frowned upon. They feel deeply that while their counterparts back home are dancing, loving, dating and enjoying themselves, they are confined in a society where there is nothing to do. This leads to intense family pressure which in many cases can lead to divorce and complete fracturing of the family.

These are problems that must be faced *before* you accept a posting to China. Don't just ask how the job will affect your career but try to sum up what it will do to your family.

If your wife is reserved and does not easily make friends or mix with strangers, a Chinese posting for you can be a personal disaster.

If she relies heavily on daily visits from her mother or friends, living in Beijing will be like being a castaway on a desert island.

And remember that Beijing or Shanghai are lively cosmopolitan places compared to most other Chinese cities. A German wife whose husband ran a factory in Qingdao described her life there as 'death before burial'. And that is in one of the most pleasant cities in the country.

Alternatives

So if your boss calls you into the boardroom and announces that you've got that big promotion and it means a two-year spell running the joint venture factory in China, don't automatically leap at the opportunity. Weigh things up. What will it mean to your family?

At different stages of your life, the scenario changes significantly.

If you are young and single, it can be that great chance to leapfrog a few rungs up the corporate ladder. Life for a single man or woman in China can be thrilling, exhilarating and exciting. True, there is a lack of singles bars and the sex life can be monotonous (or non-existent unless you happen to meet another foreigner or haunt the tourist hotel bars where visitors gather) but there are compensations. A spell in China will broaden your horizons. After all, if you can succeed in running a trade office or a factory in China, you can soar anywhere. It's a chance to prove yourself.

The picture changes drastically a few years on if you are married and have young children. How will your wife cope? First, there is the accommodation hurdle. There remains in China a vast shortage of urban housing and that applies particularly to foreigners. In big cities, it usually means living in a service apartment next to a tourist hotel. A few houses have gone up in Beijing and a big complex is planned for Shanghai. But in reality, all available decent housing has long been snapped up by companies with permanent offices in China. There is a staggering waiting list.

So your wife and children will be confined largely to an apartment.

There is likely to be a pool and health centre attached. But there will probably be little else in the way of entertainment for small children. There will be a maid to do the housework but many expatriate wives complain the presence of a person in the flat who doesn't speak a word of English and with whom communication is impossible only makes things worse. It also means she doesn't even have the chores to do to fill in those yawning empty hours when you are at the office or attending the inescapable and endless round of business banquets.

What to do? Some couples choose to separate for the period of the posting with the wife staying at home base with the children. This can be hard on a marriage. Living together in China, however, can impose even tougher burdens. Many firms give a foreign resident in China four rest and recreation trips annually to Hongkong and one of these is normally a fully-paid fare to the home city in America or Europe.

Individuals and families have to discuss things carefully and make a choice. Can their marriage survive such lengthy separations? Can it survive the stresses of living together in China?

One solution is to speak to the executive who held the job earlier. What option did he choose? How did it work out? Are there any other members of local chambers of commerce who have lived in China? If so, contact them and you will probably discover they are only too eager to recount the horror stories of their stay. As a last resort, if your boss insists you are the man for the job, say you want to go to settle in, taking your wife with you on an exploratory trip. If she likes it and, after speaking to as many foreigners as possible and discussing shopping, schools, entertainment and other aspects of life in your temporary home city, if she thinks she can bear it, she can then return with the family. She may, however, opt to stay home with the kids and impatiently await your return.

At another stage of life, when the children are grown up and a couple is mature and liberated from parenthood, a posting to China can be invigorating personally as well as professionally.

Back home, they would have been Mr and Mrs Average, senior middle management with the mortgage mostly paid off and the children working and starting families of their own, plodding along in contented middle age. But a posting to China has liberated them from the bonds of surburbia, set them free to explore a whole new life. They hurl themselves enthusiastically into China and the Chinese way of life. The wife goes busily to class to study art and language as the husband heads off to tackle production problems in a computer assembly plant or to teach at a university. For them, housing is no problem because a hotel suite is all they need. Schooling difficulties do not exist. Money is ample. And after two or three decades of being tied to the responsibility of raising children and buying a home, they have suddenly been given a new lease on an exciting fresh life. You won't hear any complaints from this group about expatriate life in China.

All the above applies in spades to retirees. For people who have ended their careers and who don't feel ready for the retirement village or the cemetery, China offers enormous opportunities for an extension to a useful lifetime. This is particularly so for management and technical experts in industry, education and agriculture who wish to serve in China in various voluntary roles. If you are interested, ask your country's foreign office for details of aid programmes in China that require volunteer staff.

Support Groups

In every city in China where there are sizeable foreign communities, local expatriate wives regularly get together for coffee and complaints. These are forums where problems rise swiftly to the surface and solutions are found. Remember, you are not Marco Polo. You are not an intrepid explorer to unknown lands breaking fresh ground. Every hurdle a newcomer faces in China has been met and overcome by people already living there. They have been in your boat—confused, perplexed, bewildered, irritated by the

unexplainable—and are pleased to soothe your fears and explain the form. If in doubt, ask.

Most communities in Beijing have clubs or associations formed around their embassies. These groups are in existence precisely to aid people like you, newcomers to China who need help. Most have published their own guides to survival in China. Don't hesitate to call your embassy to ask for help. Why else have you been paying taxes all these years?

Spouses

If you are a spouse accompanying a husband or wife on a China posting, realise from the start that life was not meant to be easy. Your husband or wife has the job to fill in at least eight hours of their day. You have to find something else to do with your time.

Without wishing to appear to be a sexist pig, life in China is easier for a jobless wife than a supported husband. Regulations make it officially impossible for a foreign spouse to take a job (although these are being relaxed) and it is a fact of life that a lone man with nothing to do to occupy his day is far more cut off from social contact than a woman. There are probably going to be a comparatively large number of wives—but few workless husbands—without jobs. The lone male will find it awkward to go to the coffee mornings with the other spouses, all of whom may be women.

For both sexes, studies provide one obvious outlet. Tutors are available to teach Chinese language, culture and cuisine. The two- or three-year posting in China can be the opportunity to open windows of learning that would otherwise never exist.

But many people keep the shutters closed tightly. They sit at home and brood, discontented malcontents. When they return home, they are full of stories of the dullness and blankness of expatriate life in China. Does fault lie with the country or with the individual who retreats snail-like into a shell?

Incidentally, some wives of Chinese diplomats who have served in New York have complained to me of the drab dullness of life in the Big Apple. It all depends on what you want from life.

The Three Burdens

The Chinese tourist industry has been likened to a gnarled old peasant climbing a steep mountain. On the back of this stooped, tortured figure there are three huge boulders. One is marked CAAC, another is labelled Bank of China and the third has written on it, China Travel Service.

These three lacklustre, incompetent and self-satisfied organisations are the major burdens carried by the tourism industry. They are heavy and distressing cargoes for an industry that should be reaping China a glowing fortune in badly-needed hard currencies. They are also the bane of visitors.

It is the opinion of some long-time China travellers that the airline, the foreign exchange offices and the travel bureaux all compete to see which can be the most inefficient, slack, rude and incompetent. It is a close-run race.

CAAC

There is a near universal agreement that CAAC is the worst airline in the world. I disagree. It is not that good. The initials stand for Civil Aviation Administration of China. Many contend they also can be read as China Aircraft Always Crash. Not all of them, of course. But a sufficient percentage manage to plough into mountains, come down in harbours or land in paddy fields to give even the bravest air traveller pause for thought.

The safety record of CAAC is truly dreadful. It is, however, considerably better than the standards of passenger services which are utterly lamentable. CAAC staff are almost invariably arrogant, high-handed, contemptuous of passengers and haughty in the extreme.

CITS

Imagine China International Travel Service is your big auntie. She's a fussy, irritable old biddy. In theory, CITS handles travel arrangements for foreign groups. She takes a very hefty commission (up to 75 per cent) for doing nothing more than making a few phone calls or issuing you a ticket.

There may well be somewhere in China a CITS office which is staffed by smiling, eager, helpful young people. If you hear of it, please let me know. In more than 60 trips to the country, I have never had reasonable service from CITS. The staff attitude is the customary slothful disdain for customers to which one soon becomes accustomed.

Despite the appalling service offered by CITS, the best advice you can have is to use them for booking your onward tickets. The alternative is to don steel Qing Dynasty armour and fight the pressing

crowds at train stations or CAAC booking offices. Having done this once, the traveller returns to the surly and arrogant CITS staff with warm feelings of brotherhood.

During one trip down to the magnificent province of Guangxi in the southwest, I had to catch an early morning train for the 34-hour journey from the local capital of Nanning to Guangzhou. The ticket had supposedly been bought and paid for by the local foreign affairs office. It had to be picked up from CITS. So on a Sunday afternoon, I found their office.

Naturally, it was locked. There was noise from inside, but nobody answered my hammerings on the stout front door. After prowling around the building, I found a rear open door. Stumbling through the unlit corridors, I eventually found the CITS office. Inside was the local tourist boss with a clutch of his cronies, watching a football match on colour television, smoking and drinking beer. Where was my ticket? Go away, he said, come back tomorrow at 9 a.m. But, I protested, the train left at midnight. Ticket, please. Go away, he waved. We're busy. I ripped the plug of the television set out of the wall, to irate disapproval. Ticket, please. Enraged, he pulled open his desk, got my ticket which was inside and hurled it at me. Then he and his pals returned to the football game.

Do not think the above example is unusual. It is run-of-the-mill service extended by CITS.

The Assignment System

You may wonder why in so many offices, shops and departments in China you constantly meet people who have, very obviously, no interest at all in what they are doing for a living. Blame the system.

One of the most hated aspects of life in modern China is the way in which people are assigned to education and jobs. The system often takes little account of where people want to spend their lives or what they wish to do. Some angry university students have complained to me about the way they were directed to study subjects

in which they had no interest and, even worse, were prevented from following the disciplines they wanted. The system is both inefficient and corrupt, a legacy of the desperate early years of the 1950s when China was striving to survive and to produce badly-needed engineers, doctors and technicians. But it has resulted in two generations of young people being forced into careers in which they have no interest. This is only too obvious to the visitor.

The system starts early. If a boy or girl is bright in middle school, they are selected for advanced studies. They may have an aptitude for mathematics but if the science and engineering quota at the local college is full, they could be directed into language, which they hate and at which they are not talented. Generally, they can list three preferences. If they are exceptionally lucky, which seems to be rare, they may get the slot they desire.

Once graduated with qualifications in a discipline in which they have little interest, the students are despatched to jobs. Once again, they are assigned to their place of work. There is no argument; they go where they are directed. In many ways, this squanders a considerable percentage of the national talent. I know one would-be chemist who was put into an English language course and who ended up as a reporter in Beijing. For many millions of young Chinese, this would be an impossible dream. For him, it's a living nightmare. He wants to be a chemist. But he is stuck with his lot. He has been assigned.

As with many aspects of modern Chinese life, there are signs of the assignment system cracking at the well-worn seams and a greater degree of freedom permitted which will give young people some say in choosing the fields in which they will spend their lives. But the educational bureaucracy is called upon to produce a certain number of technical staff for industry, a set number of nuclear scientists, a horde of language graduates speaking many tongues and graduates who are qualified in hundreds of different fields. These quotas are passed down to provincial and local levels and the result is Student Wang in Number Four Middle School in Wuhan finds himself in a science lab doing chemical experiments instead of in an arts class designing fabrics.

When student demonstrators marched in Beijing and many other cities in recent years shouting for 'democracy' and 'freedom', what they wanted changed more than anything else was the detested assignment system that moulds their lives.

Mutual Benefit

Traditional Chinese business philosophy holds that every party to a commercial agreement should make a profit. In the best of all possible worlds, this is self evident. But emerging from a commercial cocoon that has enshrouded them all their lives, young Chinese (for example, any businessman aged under 70) have never had experience about making business decisions except under the incompetent guidance of the communist system.

Here lies the rub ...

Often, Chinese state entrepreneurs are anxious to sign deals.

They sincerely want to be helpful. But there is also often a feeling that they have to squeeze out the last possible profitable dollar from a deal just to show they are as smart, as tough and as shrewd as any capitalist. The result, all too often, is that they price themselves out of the market and the foreigner who was eager to do business in China throws up his hands and relocates his factory, instead, in Thailand or the Philippines.

Instead of lamenting the lost deal, the unskilled, inept cadre is likely to give himself a pat on the back for refusing to allow himself to be fooled by the foreign plutocrat. The fact that he has lost China a badly-needed new factory will not occur to him. Such short-sighted bloody-mindedness is now not so common. But this brand of self-defeating commercial blindness can still be encountered far too frequently.

Clothing

There are few formalities in China's dress code. The very most you will ever need is a suit. Most of the time, shirtsleeves are the norm. For women, a simple dress or slacks and a jacket are adequate for anything short of an official state banquet in the Great Hall of the People. Women should not wear clothes that are excessively revealing; tank tops, for example, are embarrassing to Chinese. So are short shorts. Use your common sense.

The Mao jacket of yesteryear has largely been replaced by western-style suits and ties for senior officials. At business meetings, dress for the climate. If it's a cold day, bundle up and keep warm. If it's stifling hot, nobody will expect you to wear a jacket and tie.

When it comes to dress, the Chinese are pragmatic. Be comfortable. But not too relaxed. It's not done, for example, for men to wear shorts to official business meetings although it's perfectly acceptable to wear shorts when you are going on an inspection tour of a farm or factory.

The Other Side of the Coin

You know what you think of the Chinese you have met. What do they think of you? Probably, they are more baffled than you are.

Some people say the Chinese have a love-hate relationship with the outside world. I don't think that is strictly correct. It's more a fascination-repulsion complex.

Most Chinese have never met and spoken to a westerner. In the cities where tourists go, foreigners are no longer an item of overwhelming curiosity. They are now often taken for granted. But they are still, up close, creatures of bizarre habits, weird requests, outlandish behaviour and peculiar beliefs.

Television has given Chinese a perverted sense of the rest of the world. On the one hand, westerners are all rich beyond the dreams of any Chinese, live in splendid mansions, drive magnificent cars with gross abandon, own yachts and private aircraft and enjoy a life of perpetual excitement and glamour. With their own eyes, Chinese in Beijing and other cities witness huge Americans eat gigantic meals with disgusting amounts of meat and hardly any vegetables. Little wonder these White-skinned Ghosts are all overweight and bloated.

As any reader of *China Daily* or other newspaper can tell you, Americans are likely to have AIDS and other diseases because of their truly odious, hardly believable, sexual promiscuity and the universal habit of taking drugs. They live in cities choked with marauding gangs of criminals and oppressed minorities which are ripe for revolution. Their irresponsible government makes millions of Americans homeless and prices basic medical care well out of the reach of the sick. Many millions are unemployed, the nation is crippled by racial hatred, children defy their parents, the school system is on the point of collapse and the streets are lawless canyons roamed by armed criminals. Are you not fortunate to be a Chinese in a socialist state?

These are the contradictory viewpoints which most Chinese

have about America. There are similar glaring errors about most other nations, the result of both ignorance and propaganda. Just as you go to China with twisted notions of how they have developed, so the Chinese tend to have some astonishing ideas about the state of the rest of the world. While you will have plenty of questions to ask during your time in China, you should also expect to answer a lot. There are possibly more misconceptions about you and your way of life among the Chinese than you have about how they live.

Common Notions

Chinese tend mentally to lump all foreigners together as non-Chinese. There are exceptions. Below are some common Chinese viewpoints of different groups. These racial stereotypes are how Chinese friends in different provinces describe various nationalities to me.

I wish to stress that they are not universal Chinese viewpoints of other people. They are, however, widely held concepts and prejudices. Chinese are more ambivalent about America than about any other country. They think there is much to admire about the sheer richness and freedom of the United States while, at the same time, the greedy consumerism and unpalatable sexual and drug appetites of many Americans make most Chinese feel uncomfortable and disgusted.

Non-Chinese: Pitiful barbarians who, if they become troublesome to China, can be speedily kicked out of the country.

Americans: A generous, friendly people led by treacherous war-mongering politicians. If they are female, probably have sexual designs on innocent Chinese boys. If male, likewise, except these are on Chinese girls as well as boys.

Germans: Clever, technically brilliant people, generally hard-working, but overweight and often drunk.

French: Flamboyant and foppish, not serious but very artistic. Verging on constant anarchy.

British: Devious, tough, ruthless and brutal. Not to be trusted in any deal unless there is an obvious advantage for them that will make them keep their word.

Australians: Acceptable as business partners. Generally a rowdy, hard-drinking people.

Canadians: Nice, honest, open and generous farmers who can be trusted. Easy to do business with.

Indians: Toadies of western liberalism whose addiction to democracy makes them totally untrustworthy.

Russians: Brutal thugs itching to steal more northern territory from China. Not to be trusted.

Japanese: Suspected of ulterior motives in offers of help to develop China. Probably awaiting opportunities to rob China's riches and to control the country.

New Zealanders: Poor cousins to Australians except they get drunk faster. Always complaining about everything and saying how much better it is back home.

Blacks: Sex-crazed, drug-addicted womanisers who want to attack Chinese females. Suspected of having AIDS, black marketeering, and smuggling.

Hongkongers: Cunning Chinese in three-piece suits and haughty manners, in China to make millions by providing sophisticated industrial infrastructure. Just wait till we have them back in the fold in 1997.

Singaporean Chinese: Almost as bad as Hongkong Chinese except there are not as many of them. Too much money, too slick and smart.

Filipinos: Brown Yankees who yodel and pluck guitars. Not serious people.

Italians: Cultural robbers who stole the idea of the noodle from China and called it spaghetti. Smooth and handsome romancers who drive fast cars. Watch out for them.

Latin Americans: Victims of grasping American bankers (which makes them good guys) and conspirators who flood the world with drugs (which makes them bad guys).

Arabs: Constant tormentors of western countries who keep western barbarians occupied outside China.

Tourism

In 1978, China welcomed a grand total of 10,000 tourists. In 1988, 4,340,000 arrived. Little wonder there have been growing pains. In a decade, China has had to build 1495 new hotels and train about a million to run them. So if you have complaints (which is almost certain) there are plenty of excuses. Biggest groups of visitors in 1988 were:

	Japan	– 600,000
	USA	– 300,000
	EEC	– 422,000
	Southeast Asia	– 353,000

This does not count groups like the immense flood of Hongkong Chinese who in 1988 made more than 31 million trips over the Shenzhen River which marks the border with the homeland.

Tourism boosted China's export earnings and helped fund much development. In 1988, that totalled an impressive $2.2 billion.

The events of 1989 ended this success story. When the tanks moved in on Tiananmen, China strangled the plump goose laying lucrative golden tourist eggs. Tourism came to a crashing stop. The gleaming new foreign-run hotels that were welcoming the international camera-clicking hordes suddenly had as few people as a Tibetan glacier in winter. Officials concede grimly that it will be 1991 at the very earliest before tourist numbers edge back to the 1989 level. And that is being greatly optimistic.

CULTURAL QUIZ

CASE 1

At the hotel tour desk, you are endeavouring to find out about local excursions. The service staff is busy chatting or reading books. You say 'Excuse me' several times but they ignore you completely.

Finally you …

A Walk off in disgust.

B Slam your fist on the counter, scream 'You stupid idle fools' and demand action.

C Wait patiently then ask quietly to see the supervisor.

D Complain to the hotel management.

E Find the head office of the city tourist bureau and complain.

Answer

None of the above is likely to do you much good. I've tried all these tactics and all have ended up with a similar response, a smirk and a sneer. The temptation to lean over the counter and deliver a sharp slap around the ears is almost overwhelming but this would be the most disastrous course which would end up in a stand-up confrontation which you would be certain, one way or the other, to lose. *C* and *D* are probably the courses of action that are most likely to get you what you want, which is knowledge about city tours. *E* will probably get you lost looking for the tourism office. But complain, certainly. Write a letter on hotel notepaper and post it to the local newspaper—or, better still, *China Daily* in Beijing— describing what happened. All Chinese cities are pressing for tourism and are touchy about criticism. It mightn't help you but could result in making things a bit better for the next visitor.

CASE 2

You are at a formal dinner party. The local wine is flowing smoothly, the beer is frothing in the glass and the *mao-tai* (or provincial equivalent of the fearsome firewater) is poured evilly into tiny toasting glasses. Your host, sitting on your left, lifts a glass, raises it into the air with his right hand and touches the bottom of the glass with the fingers of his left. He is welcoming you with a respected gesture, giving you much face.

Do you:

A Say 'I don't drink' and ask for orange juice.

B Lift the identical glass that he has in his hand and return the gesture, merely touching your lips to the glass but not drinking.

C Quaff the lot with one snap of the head, say 'Terrific!' smacking your lips, and signal the waitress for more.

D Ask suspiciously 'What's this stuff?' and refuse to touch it.

Answer

A, *B* and *C* are all acceptable. If you don't touch hard liquor, that's perfectly okay. Merely explain politely to your host (the Chinese respect for the liver is similar to that of the French). Chances are, he will probably heave a hearty sigh of relief and join you with the orange soda. Most Chinese do not drink as heavily as many westerners; he may well have had to entertain a string of foreign boozers over recent days and welcomes the chance of giving his constitution a break.

On the other hand, Chinese have an almost reverent regard for the rollicking western tippler. Being obviously drunk and out of control is odious and disgraceful (as it would be in polite salon society in Europe) but enjoying a good bellyfull of beer, wine and *mao-tai* with a meal is a sign of distinction. Remember to return the toasting gesture, first to your host, then to other members of the party. Keep rank in mind and go down the list in order of importance as you rise to offer toasts between courses. Don't mind if you get precedence a bit blurred; you're only a poor benighted foreign devil, after all, and you are obviously doing your best.

CASE 3

You are a western housewife whose husband has just been sent to China. For the first time in your life, you have a maid. Unaccustomed as you are to dealing with a domestic helper, you are a bit flustered about how to treat her. She can speak only a few words of English and your lack of Chinese is total. What does she *do*? Where do her duties begin and end? How do you go about getting your relationship on a sensible working basis?

Do you ...

A   Go to your husband's office and ask his secretary or Chinese assistant to help out.

B   Take the kids for a walk and leave the servant to it.

C   Follow her around the house seeing what she does and then showing her how you want it done.

D   Contact other expatriate housewives who have lived in the city for some time, talk to them about how they solved the problem, then follow their advice.

E   Get rid of the maid and do the housework yourself.

Answer

Option *D* is probably the best course. Others have been there, done that, so profit from their experience. You'll find the maid will want to help make you happy if only because having a contented employer will make life easier for her. The problem is getting the message to her about what you want done. To start with, you've got to work out where her responsibilities start and end. Does she merely clean the house or does her employment contract include washing clothes, making beds, ironing, cooking and looking after a couple of small kids. Find out —right at the start. It's no use beginning a relationship on a basis of ignorance and later complaining that you didn't know the ground rules. Get things sorted out to your mutual agreement before she starts work. That way, there can be no confusion and no room on either side for later recriminations. *A* is not really satisfactory; it's hardly office staff job to run the home. *B* is a cop out, *C* is plain stupid (neither side will understand) and the final option will rob you of an opportunity of exploring your new environment. You're probably never going to be able to employ a maid back home in Perth or Portland, so enjoy it while you can.

CASE 4

The family is living in Beijing. There is not a great deal for teenagers to do and your son has made friends with a group of kids from the embassy compound. They seem a raucous group made up of many nationalities. You are worried about your child because he seems to be mixing with a rough crowd. This feeling of concern becomes outright fear when cocktail party gossip turns to talk of Third World diplomatic children being involved in brawls with Chinese youngsters, of shoplifting and vandalism. You talk things over with your spouse and come up with the following options.

A Send the child back home to boarding school or to live with relatives.

B Warn the lad his newfound friends are not very nice people and

have a dreadful reputation with the Chinese authorities. Ask him
to stay away from them.

C   Shrug the situation off with the comment 'Boys will be boys.'

D   Speak to officials of your country's embassy and ask for advice.

Answer

You've got a problem. The drabness of life for a foreign teenager in
Beijing is felt deeply by young people taken to live there. Parents
may find the place exciting and professionally beneficial. Young
people are unlikely to think the cultural privilege of visiting the
Forbidden City ranks with dancing in a disco back home. Many
people with teenagers who are sent to Beijing go the boarding
school route. Most companies pay for at least one passage a year for
the offspring to visit China during long school holidays. *B* is about
as likely to work in China as it is back home; best of luck. Option
C is asking for trouble. The police in Beijing have been restrained
to a remarkable extent in dealing with provocations and outright
insults by foreign children. One day, they are likely to snap, and
when they do, it will be children who are not covered by diplomatic
immunity who will bear the brunt. Option *D* is a viable alternative
if you have no choice but to keep the children in China.

CASE 5

You're starving! So are the western friends and relatives from your home country who have descended on you. They are your first house guests and you wish to impress them with the progress you've made and on how well you are settling down in China. So out you go for a meal. Of course, you've taken precautions and prepared in advance. What you have done is:

A   Nothing at all. You'll just head out and hope for the best.

B   Studied your Chinese cookbooks and phrase books so you can order dishes in your newly acquired Putonghua.

C   Spoken to Chinese friends and staff where you work and with whom you have dined before. They have telephoned the restaurant, reserved the seats and ordered the meal.

D   Booked a table at a restaurant where you know there are English-speaking staff and menus.

Answer

This is quite a good character test. If you chose *C*, you're smart, cautious and not prone to taking risks. All should be well. If you opted for *D*, this is probably equally safe but a lot more fun; at least you and your guests can look at the menu, make your decisions after discussing Chinese food and customs. Quite a civilised choice. Those who selected *B* are likely to have a good time but the chances are the waiters will not be able to understand your Chinese. Good luck. Those who picked *A* are brave folk. Best wishes to you. Chances are, all tables will be filled, nobody will understand a word you say, restaurants you remember will be closed and you'll end up back at your apartment with a bowl of soup.

It's all part of the learning experience. Remember, smile and people will fall over themselves trying to help. Point to dishes that look good. *Bon appetit!*

CASE 6

Your office has moved into a new building. You go and inspect the premises and are delighted. You have a view looking out over a wooded hillside and from your desk on the 14th floor you see directly out onto the crest of the hill.

Later, you bring your staff to the new offices and they seem less than pleased. In fact, they appear downright unhappy. Nobody will tell you what is wrong but eventually one of the staff approaches you and says the new office is in a very unlucky spot.

The 14th floor is badly selected because in Chinese the word four is pronounced *shih* which is also the way to say 'death'. And the view you so admired stares defiantly into the very eye of the dragon spirit that inhabits the hill.

How do you solve this dilemma?

A   By asking the advice of the staff, and when senior members tell you seriously to consult a geomancer to examine the situation and to suggest remedies, you follow their advice.
B   By telling the staff they are acting like a bunch of superstitious old women and to grow up?
C   By ignoring the situation.

Answer

Please, follow the first course. It may cost a couple of hundred yuan, but it is a small price to pay for peace and happiness in the office. You don't have to believe in *feng shui* yourself to take the advice of a geomancer. After the ceremony and the careful siting of chairs and desks, you can then offer roast pig and beer to the assorted spirits which have been placated before drinking and eating the offerings which have already (in a spiritual sense) been consumed by the demons and deities. After all, how does this differ all that much from the ritual western office Christmas parties?

CASE 7

You are a lucky executive. Since you have been in China running your company's joint venture plant manufacturing specialised textiles, you have heard a dozen horror stories about other expatriates whose Chinese counterparts are stiff, awkward and who insist on running their factories and offices on the old, inefficient Iron Ricebowl system. But Mr Wong, your workmate, is young, breezy, informal, a hard worker and a delight with whom to work. What's more, the factory is doing well and production schedules are well ahead of expectations.

So when Mr Wong informs you, shyly, that his wife cannot come to a reception because they are having a baby, you want to show your friendship and appreciation. What's more, you realise how important is the advent of a baby in the Chinese one-child family.

What do you choose as an instant gift for Mrs Wong?

A   A huge bowl of fruit bought from the local joint venture hotel which includes unseasonal tropical delights unobtainable in wintry China.

B   A bunch of expensive white roses flown in from the Southern Hemisphere.

C   A slinky piece of lingerie.

D   A large box of chocolates.

Answer

Buy the fruit. It will be considered a very thoughtful and welcome gesture, signifying that not only are you an appreciative boss and partner, but that you are a true friend. The flowers would be accepted with a smile by Mr Wong but never taken home to his wife. Flowers are generally offered only to the sick and having a baby is a sign of extreme good fortune. To make this gaffe worse, white is the colour of death and mourning. Chocolates would be nice but fruit is a much better choice. To give something as personal as lingerie to a Chinese woman would be disastrous. Not only would it be offensive in the extreme but would be regarded as a degrading insult.

When giving gifts to anyone on any occasion, you can't go wrong if you stick to fruit. Chinese also worship education so books are also an excellent gift. If you know a friend has a child studying a second language, a simple book in that language on some inoffensive topic such as geography or culture will be greatly appreciated.

When Chinese accept a gift, incidentally, they seldom make a great public fuss. They will often put the gift aside after a cursory glance. Don't think this means they do not like it. That's just good manners on their part.

CASE 8

The business trip has been a great success. You've been wined, dined, shown the plant and you've signed the contract. It's your last evening in China and you're trying to get away from the Chinese officials with whom you've been negotiating for the past few days so as to relax and have a few drinks. But they don't seem to take the hint and go.

What's going on?

A   Are they hanging about for some obscure reason. If so, what?

B   Do they expect some sort of gift?

C   Is there something else to do in regard to the contract?

Answer

You are being outrageously rude. When you arrived, they greeted you, welcomed you, met you at the airport and, that very first night, took you out to a welcoming banquet hosted by the most senior person in their organisation. Since then, they've taken you around, shown you the plant and sat in on negotiations and discussions.

Now it's your turn. You have to host the farewell banquet. If you fail to do so, it will brand you forever a low-born, ignorant churl and the chance of your venture succeeding will be blighted.

You should already have made arrangements for a full-scale dinner party with at least a dozen courses. You should have sought the advice of the hotel management to reserve a private dining room, on what choice local delicacies to serve, what wines to drink, what small gifts to distribute. Well before this, you should have invited them to attend a humble dinner so you could express your thanks. They are probably standing about thinking you are going to surprise them with some special function. They can't imagine you intend to merely shake hands and walk off by yourself. It's just not done.

If you had sophistication, you would have brought with you to

China some wine from your homeland (well, French wine, if you are British) and hard liquor like Scotch whisky or Bourbon. I went to an Australian banquet once where the host had the foresight to bring Australian chardonnay and rum; it was a raging victory not so much because his guests liked the drinks but because they deeply appreciated his thoughtfulness to introduce them to some delicacy from his homeland. This canny Aussie also had a couple of dozen tiny koala bears which he gave to the guests for them to give to children and grandchildren. Plus a large illustrated book on Australia for the company's reception room. He was voted an extremely civilised person.

CASE 9

For months, you have been meeting regularly with a fluent English speaker, a middle-aged man who has nothing to do with your business but whom you met in a park one day and began discussing Chinese art. It is not an intense relationship but you can relax in each other's company and you regard him as a genuine friend, one of the few you have managed to make in China.

One day, he brings along a teenager whom he introduces as his nephew. He seems a nice enough lad. The next time you meet, your friend asks you, at first hesitantly, then bluntly, then insistently, what you can do to help the boy go to your native land to study at university. You attempt to shrug off the approach but it becomes obvious at future meetings you are seriously expected to act. You feel embarrassed and upset. Your friend has used your relationship in an attempt to manipulate you into a situation you wish to avoid. He is trying to cash in on your goodwill.

What to do?

A Agree that the boy should go abroad to study and do your best to help obtain a scholarship, university place and a student visa for your homeland.

B Tell your friend, bluntly, that you are upset because he is using

your friendship to try to obtain favours which, anyway, you are in no position to obtain.

C Shout your outrage and say the friendship is ended and you never want to see anyone in the family ever again.

D Advise the boy to apply through normal channels at your consulate, offering to pick up the application papers for him and to ask for printed information about universities back home.

Answer

Welcome to the land of *guanxi*. Your artistic friend sees nothing wrong at all in his behaviour. After all, you are friends and friends are meant to help each other whenever possible. And his nephew is family. So helping his nephew is the same as helping him. Why are you upset? Don't you understand?

Under no circumstances agree to the first choice. This is like leaping into quicksand. As soon as the youth is on the plane overseas, approaches will be made to you to aid his sister or some other relative or a friend to join him. It's the start of a slippery slope, indeed. Much as you may want to help, once you start you will be inundated by requests. Virtual strangers will approach you; if you've got a reputation of being a soft touch who can get things done, half of China will besiege you seeking educational placement abroad.

I strongly advise taking the last course. There's little chance, unless you've got personal pull with your country's Minister of Education, of helping someone jump the queue. It's a lengthy bureaucratic process and the forms have to be filled out, considered back in your homeland, the I's dotted and the T's crossed. It can't hurt to get a couple of dozen forms from your embassy and give them to friends, but stress absolutely you have no *guanxi* back home with the authorities and there is nothing more you can do to help. You will then probably be asked to sponsor or guarantee a student financially. This, of course, is up to you. I have had people I hardly know approach me asking that I pay several thousand dollars to sponsor someone to study abroad and sign guarantees that I will pay their medical expenses, plane fares back to China and other commitments. No way. Sorry about that, but no, no, no.

Chinese will then look at you mournfully and say: 'But I thought you were my friend.' This may hurt your feelings. It will hurt you a lot more if you wade into this mire. I did help, once, to get the son of a close friend to apply for a visa. What I did was nothing more than pick up application forms and help fill them out. I was then virtually surrounded by supplicants for weeks asking that I help their relatives, and their relatives' friends, and their relatives' friends' friends. And so it went on.

Choices *B* and *C* may seem rough. You may be tempted to resort to them. Don't. Why should you, on the basis of a casual acquaintanceship, be held responsible for making a serious economic and financial commitment? No reason at all. Don't let yourself be suckered by guilt and sympathy into doing so. You'll only be making trouble for yourself in the future. Firmly stick to Choice D and advise them to go through the normal procedure.

CASE 10

Walking out of the hotel for a post-dinner stroll, you are approached by a youth who whispers loudly: 'Change money?' You have no intention of breaking the strict economic law that forbids changing money anywhere but with an official bank or when purchasing goods at a recognised shop. But the young man is insistent. Finally, you ask him the rate. Officially US$10 is worth $37.13 in Foreign Exchange Certificates. Under the law, these are worth exactly the same as the Renminbi. But this fellow is offering you almost double the official rate.

You are sorely tempted. Do you:

A Agree and follow him into a doorway to make the exchange.
B Say loudly 'No thank you' and walk on.
C Bargain with him to try to get an even better rate.

Answer

It's up to you. Moneychangers are present in just about every city, hanging around the entrances of tourist hotels and in streets frequented by foreigners. The standard rate seems to be roughly 80 per cent more than the official rate. You give them foreign currency and they pay you in RMB. But beware; by dabbling with street moneychangers you are breaking the law. I've never heard of a genuine tourist ever being charged but now and again some local coppers will suffer a rush of blood to the head and will launch a crackdown. The police authorities must be aware of these touts and the way they make a living—Chinese policemen are not stupid—and I have no doubt they keep a watch on them.

Touts are touts are touts anywhere. I've heard of some short-charging tourists. If you are robbed, what are you going to do? Go to the local Public Security Bureau and lodge a complaint, admitting that you broke the law?

This is a moral, ethical and legal decision you are going to have to make on your own. You know the benefits (and everyone wants to double his money) but you must also appreciate the risks. If you think it's worth it, that's up to you. However, don't blame anyone but yourself if you are caught—which is extremely unlikely—and charged.

BIBLIOGRAPHY

It is impossible to publish a full bibliography of works on China. Such a list would itself fill a sizeable volume. In recent years, hundreds of books have been written about many aspects of life in modern China.

Here is a list of suggested books that give readers a grasp of China today. For a start, I suggest that anyone who wants to understand the nation today reads the classic *Red Star Over China* written in 1937 by American newspaperman Edgar Snow. He risked his life (with my old friend, George Hatem, better known as Dr Ma Haide) to penetrate the Kuomintang cordon around the communist area of Yanan in Shaanxi to meet the shadowy Mao Zedong and the Red Army shortly after they finished the epic journey which has gone down in history as the Long March. It was Snow's explosive book that first told the world about the communists, who they were and what they meant to do. The aspirations expressed by Mao and other leaders like Chu Deh, Chen Yi, Liu Shaoqi, He Long and Zhou Enlai laid the framework for the modern state.

A Guide to the Guidebooks

Since China opened its doors to tourists in 1978, a number of guide books have been regularly published. Most are comprehensive volumes which divide China by provinces and give tips on what to see, where to stay, what to eat and general outlines of the country and some of its customs. Almost all are intended for the casual visitor rather than those who plan to spend a lot of time in China.

My favourite is *China; A Travel Survival Tip* which injects a bit of badly needed humour in its wry observations. Prices have not been included because these change from country to country.

Guide Books

China; A Travel Survival Kit. Alan Samagalski and Michael Buckley, Lonely Planet, California, USA, 1984.

The China Guidebook, 1984 edition. Fredric M. Kaplan/Arne J. de Keijzer, Eurasia Press, New York, USA, 1984.

The China Guidebook, 1989 edition. Fredric M. Kaplan, Julian M. Sobin/Arne J. de Keijzer, Eurasia Press, New York, USA, 1988.

The Rough Guide to China. Researched and written by Catherine Sanders, Chris Stewart and Rhonda Evans, Routledge & Kegan Paul Ltd, London, UK, 1987.

Through the Moon Gate, A guide to China's Historic Monuments. Edited by the China People's Publishing House of Fine Arts, Oxford University Press, Hongkong, 1986.

60 Scenic Wonders in China. Edited by The Editorial Department of New World Press and The English Language Service of Radio Beijing, New World Press, Beijing, China, 1980.

Fielding's People's Republic of China 1989. Ruth Lor Malloy, Fielding Travel Books, New York, USA, 1975.

The China Business Handbook. Arne J. de Keijzer, Asia Business Communications Ltd, Weston, CT and China Books & Periodicals, Inc., California, USA, 1986.

China, the Encyclopedia-Guide. Nagel Publishers, 1978.

Fodor's Guide to Beijing, Guangzhou and Shanghai. John Summerfield, 1984.

Economy, China Handbook Series. Compiled by the China Handbook Editorial Committee, Foreign Languages Press, Beijing, China, 1984.

Geography, China Handbook Series. Compiled by the China Handbook Editorial Committee, Foreign Languages Press, Beijing, China, 1983.

Handbook for China. Carl Cow, Oxford University Press, 1933.

General Reading

Travels in Tartary, Tibet and China, 1844–1846. Evariste-Regis Huc and Joseph Gabet, Dover Publications, Inc. New York, USA, 1987.

Red Star Over China, by Edgar Snow.

Forgotten Tribes of China. Kevin Sinclair, Intercontinental Publishing Corporation Ltd, Hongkong, 1987.

The Yellow River. Kevin Sinclair, Intercontinental Publishing Corporation Ltd, Hongkong, 1987.

Over China. Kevin Sinclair, Intercontinental Publishing Corporation Ltd, Hong Kong, 1988.

Chronological Handbook of the History of China. Dr E. Faber, Shanghai, 1902.

Imperial Life in the Qing Dynasty. Edited by Grace Wong and Goh Eck Kheng, Historical and Cultural Exhibitions Pte Ltd, Singapore.

Spectrum of Chinese Culture. Lee Siow Mong, Pelanduk Publications (M) Sdn Bhd, Malaysia, 1987.

China, Land of Discovery and Invention. Robert K.G. Temple, Patrick Stephens Limited, UK, 1986.

Outlines of Chinese Symbolism & Art Motives. C.A.S. Williams, Dover Publications, Inc., New York, USA, 1976.

Chinese Mythology. Anthony Christie, The Hamlyn Publishing Group Limited, Middlesex, UK, 1968.

Confucius. Editor-in-Chief, Miao Fenglin, Shandong Provincial General Publishing House, Shandong Pictorial, Shandong Province, China, 1989.

The Essence of Chinese Civilization. Dun J. Li, D. Van Nostrand Company, New York, USA, 1967.

Your Chinese Roots, the Overseas Chinese Story. Thomas Tsu-wee Tan, Times Books International, Singapore, 1986.

China Modernisation and its Economic Laws. Peter P.F. Chan, The Hong Kong Economist Newspaper Limited, Hongkong, 1982.

This is China, Analyses of Mainland Trends and Events. Edited by Francis Harper, Dragonfly Books, Hongkong, 1965.

A Land of Fascination, The Definitive Guide for Travel to Hangzhou and Zhejiang Province. Edited by He Qi, People's Publishing House, Zhejiang Province, China, 1987.

The Handbook of Chinese Horoscopes. Theodora Lau, Arrow Books, London, UK, 1979.

The Fontana Collection of Modern Chinese Writing. Edited by Christine Liao, Fontana/Collins Books Australia, in association with The Chinese Literature Publishing House of Beijing, Beijing, China, 1983.

China, Old and New. John Logan, Publications Division, South China Morning Post, Hongkong, 1982.

Best Chinese Idioms, Volume 1. Compiled by Situ Tan, Hai Feng Publishing Company, Hongkong, 1986.

Best Chinese Idioms, Volume 2. Compiled by Situ Tan, Hai Feng Publishing Company, Hongkong, 1988.

The Chinese People's Liberation Army, From the Long March to the Hydrogen Bomb. Samuel B. Griffith II, Weidenfeld and Nicolson, London, UK, 1967.

Chinese Temples and Deities. Evelyn Lip, Times Books International, 1986.

Proverbs and Common Sayings from the Chinese. Arthur Smith, Paragon Book Reprint Corp. and Dover Publications, Inc., New York, USA, 1965.

A Collection of Chinese Proverbs. Rev. W. Scarborough and Rev. C. Wilfrid Allan, Paragon Book Reprint Corp., New York, USA, 1964.

The Great Chinese Revolution 1800–1985. John King Fairbank, Harper and Row, New York, USA, 1986.

Chinese Cavalcade. Kwan Kim-Gaul, Herbert Jenkins Limited, London, UK, 1963.

Recent Discoveries in Chinese Archaeology. Edited by Foster Stockwell and Tang Bowen, The Foreign Languages Press, Beijing, China, 1984.

China—A Short Cultural History. C.P. Fitzgerald, Praeger (1935) 1961.

Mao Tse Tung. S. Schram.

Red China Today: The Other Side of the River. Edgar Snow, Penguin, 1970.

The Arts of China. Michael Sullivan, Cardinal, 1973.

Dragon by the Trail. John Paton Davies, Robson.

Morrison of Peking. Cyril Pearl, Angus and Robertson.

The Chinese. David Bonavia.

Deng. David Bonavia, Longman Group (Far East) Limited, Hongkong, 1989.

Coming Alive—China After Mao. Roger Garside, Deutch.

China After Mao: China's Second Revolution. Harry Harding, Washington, Brookings Institute, 1987.

China the Beautiful Cookbook. Kevin Sinclair, IPC.

Scrutable Chinese Cooking. Kevin Sinclair and Lily Levin, Lily's Way Inc., 1984.

THE AUTHORS

KEVIN SINCLAIR has been a leading Hongkong newspaperman for more than 20 years. The New Zealand-born reporter is senior columnist on *The Hongkong Standard* and chief correspondent for *China Review* magazine. He has also written a number of international bestselling books on Hongkong, the South China Sea and China, dealing with history, culture, anthropology, salvage, peoples and cuisine. In 1983, Sinclair was made a Member of the Order of the British Empire for his services to journalism in Hongkong.

Iris Wong Po-yee is a Hongkong reporter who has made many visits to China. A graduate in English literature from Hongkong Baptist College, she is a fluent speaker of both Cantonese and Putonghua. A freelance journalist whose byline appears in many regional and international magazines, Wong is particularly interested in the economic and social development of the southern regions of China. She has worked as a researcher for numerous books dealing with the politics, geography and history of the country.

Iris Wong and Kevin Sinclair

INDEX